THE
UNCHARTED
JOURNEY

THE
UNCHARTED
JOURNEY

EXPLORING
THE INNER LANDSCAPE

DON ROSENTHAL

A LIVING PLANET BOOK

STERLING ETHOS
An imprint of Sterling Publishing Co., Inc.

New York / London
www.sterlingpublishing.com

Dedicated with love and awe to Martha,
my beloved wife and traveling companion of thirty-eight years.

Deepest thanks to Kate Zimmermann, David Nelson, and the folks at Sterling, and to Josh Horwitz and Patty Gift for believing in this book from the beginning. I am grateful to J. Krishnamurti, for being the first teacher to break through my formidable barriers; to Nisargedatta Maharaj, Hubert Benoit, Robert Hall, Eckhart Tolle, Byron Katie, and many others who helped deepen my understanding; to Helen Shucman, Pat Rodegast, Mary Margaret Moore, and Esther Hicks, whose capacity to access the purest wisdom was a blessing on my journey. I am grateful to Michael Lavender, my dear friend, whose passion for enquiry in our many long conversations helped shape my ideas for this book; to Dan Breslaw, whose continuing friendship, highest quality editing skills, and persistent devotion helped bring me the needed clarity to hone my thoughts and to see the project through; and to my dear son Aram, an inspiration at every level.

STERLING and the distinctive Sterling logo are registered
trademarks of Sterling Publishing Co., Inc.

Library of Congress Cataloging-in-Publication Data

Rosenthal, Don.
The uncharted journey : exploring the inner landscape / Don Rosenthal.
p. cm.
ISBN 978-1-4027-4475-4 (alk. paper)
1. Self psychology. 2. Self-actualization (Psychology)—Religious aspects. I. Title.
BF697.R65745 2009
158.1—dc22   2008040692

1   3   5   7   9   10   8   6   4   2

Published by Sterling Publishing Co., Inc.
387 Park Avenue South, New York, NY 10016
© 2009 by Don Rosenthal
Distributed in Canada by Sterling Publishing
℅ Canadian Manda Group, 165 Dufferin Street
Toronto, Ontario, Canada M6K 3H6
Distributed in the United Kingdom by GMC Distribution Services
Castle Place, 166 High Street, Lewes, East Sussex, England BN7 1XU
Distributed in Australia by Capricorn Link (Australia) Pty. Ltd.
P.O. Box 704, Windsor, NSW 2756, Australia

Sterling ISBN 978-1-4027-4475-4

For information about custom editions, special sales, premium and
corporate purchases, please contact Sterling Special Sales
Department at 800-805-5489 or specialsales@sterlingpublishing.com.

CONTENTS

INTRODUCTION—
THE PATHLESS LAND

SURVEYING THE TERRITORY

What is it we want?

In this deceptively simple question lurks one of the most profound paradoxes of our existence. We all feel a deeply intuitive wish to be happy, to be at peace, to lead lives of richness and fulfillment. Yet in our struggles to achieve these ends, we often find ourselves caught in tangles of frustration and conflict. Often it seems that the harder we struggle, the greater our suffering. The more we hold up to ourselves the vision of peace and joy that we believe to be our birthright, the more agonizing the realization that this is not the reality, that we are somehow falling short. Our grasping at happiness seems to lead to its opposite, to a profound dissatisfaction with ourselves, our lives, and our world.

Is there a way out of this dilemma? Surprisingly, in view of how intractable the problem can seem, the answer is Yes. For several millennia now, teachers and sages from many different cultures and spiritual traditions have been conveying the message that there is, indeed, a way to move toward true peace and harmony: by changing our consciousness rather than our circumstances. The pursuit of this way is often described as a spiritual path or journey. Probably no metaphor is more common in spiritual literature. But what are the implications of the metaphor? If we are on a path, may we not inquire where the path is taking us? How does one begin it? How do we know when we are on it and when we are not? Does it have a destination, an end point that we would recognize upon arrival? Is there but one path, or are there many? Are there "false" paths, and, if so, how do we detect them? Most perplexing of all, what differentiates a spiritual path from our usual efforts to better ourselves and our circumstances? How can we know it isn't simply more of the same futile grasping after the will-o'-the-wisp we call happiness?

Questions like these never cease to pose their subtle but powerful challenge, conveying the paradoxical flavor inherent in any deep inquiry. To speak of an "uncharted journey" suggests that there is an end, or goal, toward which we are moving; but it also suggests the sense that this goal cannot be located on any map of existence that we know of. To get anywhere at all, we must throw away the map and surrender to the mysterious logic of the journey itself. Every time we think we have a fix on exactly where we are along the way, how much "progress" we have made, or how close we are to the journey's destination, the cloudiness of the terrain has a way of plunging us back into doubt and uncertainty. Which is what makes the whole topic so deeply fascinating.

It is not until one has actually tried to live the spiritual life that one comes to understand the curious restrictions, anomalies, and befuddlements to which such a life subjects us. When I was younger and first embarking on the path, I was excited to think that I had gained (with the help of a few sages) a handle on the deepest riddles of existence. It was comforting to believe that my sole requirement henceforth would be to conduct myself according to my new and enlightened perspective. Gradually I discovered that it was not so simple. I came to see that any belief I had in my own spiritual accomplishments was probably misplaced, that such a belief only got in the way of my understanding, and that the only way to make any headway at all was to relinquish whatever assumptions I had about who I was or where I was going.

The paradox, of course, is that having been thus humbled by life, I do feel better able to address some of the important questions it poses. What is the actual nature of the spiritual quest for us, the human beings pursuing it? What does it really mean—not just in theory, but in practice—to make such a quest the guiding principle of one's life? What does it mean moment-to-moment, in our lives, our work, our relationships? Here is where interesting challenges come into play.

One of these challenges stands out above all. Spiritual teachings from time immemorial have spoken of the need to be free from the illusion of a separate self, free from the ego-mind at the source of all our discomfort. They advise us to be aware, to free ourselves from egoic thought and judgment, to be lovingly present for each moment. Though I have no doubt about the desirability of all this, I confess that I find it sometimes quite challenging. A whole range of obstacles presents itself— not the least of them my own struggle to attain this state. It's easy for me to say there is value in bringing compassion or

presence to each moment, yet I often find both sorely wanting. Though the old mind's interpretation tells me I "should"
be lovingly present, the very existence of that "should" both
signifies and creates a closed heart and further conflict. If a distracted, unloving mind is part of what is, how do I greet it? Do
I battle it as an enemy? Do I accept it and resign myself to its
reign of confusion and darkness? Or is there yet another way
to hold it, different from both of these?

This conundrum appears in one way or another at the heart of
all spiritual struggle. In the course of my reading I have come
across books on spiritual topics that pointed me toward where
I wished to be and described an essential means to get there,
but were not overly helpful in addressing the specific obstacles
in the way. My hope is that this book—which I think of as a
kind of "applied" spirituality—may assist in filling that gap.
However compelling the vision of perfection offered by spiritual teachings, it is the investigation of the obstacles to realizing that vision, the exploration of *im*perfection, that deeply
absorbs me. This is natural, since most of my spiritual learning
has been around my own imperfections. It is also convenient
for me as an author, as I sense that my imperfections are not so
different from those of others. Hence this book, while based
wholly on my own experience, is addressed to those who have
chosen to wrestle with the same spiritual dilemma. Our path
may be full of obstacles, but the obstacles, in a way, *are* the path.
They are what teach us. It is therefore worth paying a great
deal of attention to them.

Despite all my disclaimers, then, I am, after all, offering a sort of
"map" of the spiritual terrain to those who wander it with me.
I offer it at least in the sense of saying to the reader:"Here are

some of the difficulties I have encountered along the way. Perhaps you have experienced similar ones. If so, you may find
interest in hearing about mine and how I have addressed
them." To put it this way is to acknowledge that the spiritual
path is no marked trail, but rather a winding, muddled set of
tracks through a mysterious landscape. The ultimate guide is
one's always-present deeper wisdom, the wisdom of the True
Self.

The Uncharted Journey, then, is in a sense a journey with no
known destination. But we know for certain where it begins:
wherever we happen to be. To set foot upon it requires but
one important realization: that the source of happiness cannot
be sought "out there," but only within; that the way the mind
holds experience is overwhelmingly more important in determining our well-being than the specific nature of that experience. This is the central insight; the rest of the journey is
merely a discovery and elaboration of its truth. Which means
that the journey itself, despite the many stories its travelers
have to tell, is in some way the same for all who embark upon
it. Though it may not lead to a goal the mind can recognize, it
leads us through landscapes invariably familiar to our fellow
sojourners.

Why write this book, then, if the territory described is so well
trodden? I have thought about this question a great deal, for it
is a legitimate one. Thousands of books have been written
about the rewards and challenges of the spiritual life. Is there a
need for one more? My qualified answer is: perhaps. In addition to what I have mentioned—that more (perhaps endlessly
more) remains to be said about the obstacles standing in the
way of a "spiritual" life—there is also value in appreciating the

uniqueness of our paths. Despite the similarity of the landscape, there is an unmistakably personal pattern to any spiritual journey, a pattern that differs with each individual and can be as distinctive as a fingerprint or a snowflake. It's true that the spiritual aspect of our nature is what we share in common with others, the part that is universal. Yet we each come to this common truth from our individual confusions, from our tangled histories, and from the messy complexity of our personalities. We all make our way through the bewildering diversity of our individual lives to the realm of the One Truth.

My own journey, undertaken some forty years ago, has taken me through many twists and turns and led me to many interesting places, both geographical and spiritual. Some of these places will be recognizable to readers who have been on journeys of their own; others are more distinctively mine. But it is always helpful to know some of the history behind an author's reflections: if nothing else, it reminds us that our perception of Truth is always to some extent influenced by human factors. And yet, taken together, our individual stories are part of a greater collective story that stands before us as both inspiration and reference point.

What follows, then, is my own "story": how I came to enter on the path, the direction in which that path has taken me, the main contours of the landscape I have encountered, and where it has brought me today.

AN ABRUPT AWAKENING

In 1968, I was living in a small cabin outside of Fairbanks, Alaska. It was to be the scene of a major turning point in my life—one I could not have anticipated or prepared for, though from my present vantage point it seems almost inevitable. I had come to Alaska some five years earlier, having abandoned the East Coast and a career as a classical bassoonist. Even as a musician, I had led a somewhat adventurous life. Unencumbered by family or commitments, I had traveled throughout America, Europe, Russia, and South America, playing with top-caliber symphony orchestras and chamber music groups and receiving my share of recognition and applause. I encountered interesting people of all sorts and developed many friendships, both intimate and otherwise. I spent plenty of time in bars and other arenas of recreation, using copious quantities of alcohol and other drugs to enhance my pleasures. I had leisure to roam mountains, forests, and seashores, soaking up their beauty and inspiration. In short, I had become the consummate hedonist, deeply engrossed in my pleasures and oblivious to any other calling in life.

Playing across the surface of this life, however, was a shadow. Whatever I did, I always had the feeling of staving off boredom or dissatisfaction. Rather than fully enjoying my pleasures, I found myself anticipating future ones, as if they represented where my true satisfaction would lie. Thus when a concert tour of Alaska with the New York Woodwind Quintet brought me a glimpse of a spectacular land inhabited by fascinating people (many of them mavericks, as I fancied myself to be), I made a sudden decision to give up my old life. With everything I owned packed into the back seat of my Volkswagen, I drove nearly six thousand miles from New York to Homer, Alaska, on the shores of Kachemak Bay. There, at the farthest point on the highway system, I found myself in the midst of one of the world's most spectacularly beautiful landscapes.

Initially, this new life seemed to promise everything I had sought. In Alaska, I experienced an excitement that made my old existence seem tame and limited. The people I met were as fascinating as I had suspected they would be. When I moved temporarily to Fairbanks to finish my college degree, I quickly established a whole circle of interesting friends, many of them as devoted to the good life as I was. I was able to earn a living by giving only a few hours of music lessons each week, leaving me abundant time for relaxation, conversation, and excursions into the wilderness, where I was enthralled by the wildness and silence of nature. There were all sorts of adventures to be had, and I was hopeful that the growing emptiness would finally be filled.

On one such adventure, a companion and I were dropped off by bush plane in mid-winter in the midst of the Alaska Range, where temperatures can get down to 70 below. Over a hundred miles from the nearest settlement, equipped only with a compass and a map marked with scribbles, we spent the few hours of daily sunlight skiing through the mountains from remote cabin to remote cabin. For a few days I felt superbly alive. Playing at the edge of my wilderness capability—taking what was probably, in retrospect, a serious risk with my life—I experienced an excitement I had never known. Following that was the pleasurable relief as the plane finally approached the crude mountain landing strip, and still later, the satisfaction of swaggering into the Fairbanks airport like a wild man. Nevertheless, like all my other pleasures, these feelings faded all too swiftly and I was left with the familiar burden of either replacing them with still more excitement or facing the emptiness itself.

•   •   •

Despite the endless delights available to me, things weren't quite working as I had planned. My new life was by all measures a success, and yet I had to acknowledge that something was still wrong. In the back of my mind, I suspected that no matter what new pleasures I devised for myself, they would always pall; to dispel my dissatisfaction, I would always be seeking something more. Could that dissatisfaction be part of me, rather than something amiss in my circumstances? Could it be something I had always carried inside me, even back East—something I had brought to Alaska along with my other belongings? Would I carry it forever? Was this really all there was to life?

In retrospect, I think that at that point, in my little cabin outside Fairbanks in 1968, I was only half-conscious of the malaise that had been eating at me. In any case, I was certainly oblivious to the enormous psychic upheaval that was looming just ahead.

It began casually enough. One evening, I picked up a book that had been collecting dust on my table. "Krishnamurti isn't too fond of sex and drugs," my friend had said, grinning, when she lent me the book, "but you might enjoy this anyway." Now I looked at the author's face on the cover, its expression somehow mingling calm strength with kindness, and was inexplicably intrigued by the wisdom it seemed to betoken. Why not, I thought. I opened a beer, sat back on the couch, and began to read.

After a few pages, my interest began to mix with bafflement. I was usually swift to judge other people's thoughts, glibly categorizing them as either true and intelligent or the reverse; but this was a perspective altogether outside the realm of thought. Although the book was written simply enough, in the form of a dialogue, I couldn't wrap my mind around the meaning of the author's words. They were unlike anything I had encountered.

In the middle of a page, a questioner asked the author if it wasn't difficult to be present in the moment. He answered: "Yes, it is, when there is thought."

I stopped reading. Here was someone suggesting that an entire universe lay waiting in the silence beyond thought. What could that possibly mean? What could be "beyond" thought? Thought was the realm in which I had always lived—in which everybody lived, of necessity. There couldn't be anything beyond it. Or could there?

I suddenly felt as if I had been punched in the stomach. For a moment my own thoughts totally ceased. In the interval of silence there arose a powerful, wordless understanding. Then I realized that this feeling was connected to another experience I had had a few days earlier, which now came back to me in a vivid flash. I had stepped outside into the frigid Fairbanks night. The almost-full moon cast a mysterious light on the silent, sub-arctic landscape. Something about the stillness and beauty had caused my usual inner chatter to quiet; what remained was the intensity of the silence itself. I stood there transfixed, gazing at the moon, the stars, and the landscape from a wholly different place. It was as though "I" no longer existed; there was only . . . this. Had I been a religious person, it would have felt like a holy moment. Then, after a timeless interval, it was over. I turned and went back inside, gratified to have had a moving experience (one more pleasure), and thought no more about it.

Now, as my attention returned to this rather unusual book I was reading, I suddenly knew what had happened to me that night. I understood the difference between being present with thought and being truly present in silence. I grasped the vastness of the world that opened up to me when thought was stilled. It was no less than my whole life—which, as long as I was lost in my thoughts, I was missing. It was a shock to realize that I was hardly even experiencing the pleasurable and adventurous existence I prized so greatly. Instead I was experiencing my thoughts *about* that existence.

I recalled the times I had been touched deeply by an experience. I thought of listening in wonder to my favorite works of music, the late string quartets of Beethoven. When I was distracted, when my mind was busy, these great works of art were mere background music. Only when the mind was still could I fully experience their sublimity. This, I realized, was a picture of my life. I saw that as long as thought was present, I was somewhere else—and thought was almost always present. Whether eating, talking with friends, walking in the hills, listening to music, or watching the sunset, what I was really doing in all these moments was *thinking*. I was hardly conscious of my surroundings, hypnotized by my own thoughts, walking about in a state of waking sleep.

I was appalled by this revelation. No wonder my satisfactions were so fleeting, my life so unfulfilling. What was required was a fundamental change, something far more basic than my circumstances. It couldn't be anything "out there"; it had to be something inside me. Without quite understanding all the implications, I experienced a powerful urge to wake up.

The following days, weeks, and months were like no others I had experienced. Without any exact plan but driven by a ferocious intensity, I began to transform my life. A friend and I had purchased eighty acres of land a remote distance from my old haunts, reachable only on foot, and had built a six-by-nine-foot sauna to shelter us while we erected a larger cabin. I decided this would be the perfect setting for my quest. I moved into the tiny space in the late summer, and remained there until the following spring.

Winter arrived, as it does in northern Alaska, in late September. Day by day, temperatures plummeted and darkness lengthened. Except for occasional trips for supplies, I stopped going to town and ceased all social activities. My desire for chemical support dropped away. I began to spend long days and nights just sitting still, looking within, investigating the challenge that had been presented to me. My activity—or rather inactivity—seemed to be encouraged by the long Alaskan winter darkness, which increased by seven minutes each day. I had never been a person of moderation; that, at least, was to remain a constant. I spent countless silent hours in the tiny sauna, much of it in total darkness, pushing the inner quest as far as I was able, awaiting I knew not what. I lost interest in all other activity, wishing only to find out what lay beyond the realm of thought. I burned with questions: What is going on in this moment? Is there something "wrong" with it? Who is watching it all? What is the reality of time? None of these questions could be answered by thinking. All I could do was try to pay attention to what was happening in each moment. At some point I realized that what I was doing was "meditating."

One day, after many hours of sitting in silence, I decided to take a break. Walking along a narrow, mossy animal trail through an area of scrubby spruce, I gave up trying to force my mind in any special direction and began simply to appreciate my surroundings. The last actual thought I can remember was "I wonder why I call this arm 'me,' but that tree over there 'not me.'" Then, relaxed from all its focused intensity, my mind entered an effortless state free from thought—free even from the attempt not to think—following some natural flow of its own.

All at once an inner explosion occurred, unlike anything I had ever experienced. The curtains of ignorance seemed to part magically, and consciousness opened into a realm entirely beyond what the mind had known or could know. At the time I had read none of the world's spiritual literature. Only later did I realize that what had happened was a recognizable "spiritual" or "mystical" experience, not unlike those described by countless individuals from many different cultures over thousands of years.

As many recalling these experiences have said, words can merely hint at what is seen. I saw that the being I called "me," or "Don Rosenthal," had no reality—or, rather, that its reality was like a dream from which one might awaken. With the vanishing of this illusion of a separate self, I saw clearly that "I" was simply Life, the one Life Force at the heart of a universe that included people, animals, plants, planets, stars, all matter and energy, all that is. Since there was only this One, it could never be extinguished, although the form through which it expressed itself changed endlessly. Because my true being rested in this vast oneness, which could never be hurt, threatened, or destroyed, I saw that death was unreal. With this, all cause for fear vanished at every level. With the ending of fear arose what was clearly my natural state: a love beyond description, along with a pervasive sense of peace, joy, and perfect clarity. An utter sacredness enveloped me, of which I was a part. The whole experience was stamped with a sense of rightness and truth that to this day feels more real and compelling than my "normal" consciousness right now as I write these words.

After what seemed like a timeless interval (but was probably several hours by the clock), the familiar sense of self gradually returned and I once again found myself in the world of illusion that had preceded my experience; and yet nothing was quite the same. Nor, for that matter, has it ever been the same in the forty years since. What lingered was the afterglow from that blazing moment of illumination, serving as a beacon, giving my life a direction and purpose it had never had before.

My experience brought into focus a few basic truths: On the one hand, there is much suffering, both in my consciousness and in the world. On the other, things are not what they seem, outwardly and inwardly; my mind's perception is not reality. I began to see a profound relationship between these two facts. I saw that it is possible to perceive things as they are, and that in so doing, suffering will end. The only meaningful goal for me now was to pursue this clear seeing with all the intelligence and passion I could muster. I could do this only by being fully present for my life.

Following that winter, my life began to move along a different arc. I remained in Alaska, but my focus had shifted from the accumulation of pleasures to what felt like a serious inner exploration. For a while, I abandoned all ordinary pursuits and lived alone in a series of cabins, where I could practice meditation and continue my inner work. I simplified my life, spending long stretches of time alone. I took up yoga and experimented with fasting and radical diets. I began to read the world's spiritual literature, devouring much of it (at least, the parts that resonated for me) voraciously. My conversations with friends took on a different flavor, probably more so than some of them appreciated. I was a man on a mission, with only one goal in my life: to grasp the mystery at the heart of existence.

But there would be yet more twists along the path . . .

A few years into my new existence, I met Martha, who was also living alone on the Alaskan coast. We were powerfully drawn to one another, but still I was wary. Entanglement with a woman seemed like the last thing I needed, a terrible distraction from my single-minded, solitary pursuit of enlightenment. Yet here was a woman whose desire for truth seemed to match my own. It was a terrible conflict. Fortunately, healthy instinct triumphed over abstract reasoning, and Martha and I entered into a partnership that, over the next three-plus decades, would become one of the defining influences of my life, as well as its greatest blessing.

·   ·   ·

Our solitude became a solitude of two. For the next few years, Martha and I spent almost all of our time together, living simply in a series of small cabins, practicing yoga and meditation, and having long, soulful conversations about our inner lives. As yet not quite able to shake our faith in the value of exotic experience, we embarked (like so many in those days) on a year-long spiritual pilgrimage to the East. We hitchhiked across the country, then flew to Europe, where we taught at the Krishnamurti School in England and spent the summer in a barn in the Swiss Alps, attending an annual gathering held by Krishnamurti and his students. We then took a series of buses and other conveyances across the exotic and sometimes dangerous expanse of Asia from Europe to Nepal, where, upon finally arriving, we trekked for nine days into the Himalayas until we reached a tiny village high up in the world's steepest valley. There we took up residence in a small hut and hunkered down to meditate. Surely, we thought, immersing ourselves in this breathtaking environment, together with receiving the inspiration of a spiritually rich culture, would bring us the fulfillment we craved.

Often we would sit together as the sun went down, gazing in peaceful contemplation at the outlines of Annapurna and Dhaulagiri, the two giants on either side of the valley, rising above us in glowing splendor. On one such evening, a group of Tibetan travelers suddenly appeared along the ridge, dressed in colorful traditional costumes. Martha and I watched them in awe. "It doesn't get any better than this," I thought to myself as they moved slowly toward us in single file.

The sun went down, and we returned in silence to our hut. There we discovered that we had both come to the same unexpected realization: no experience, however intense, exotic, or otherwordly, could ever make a real difference in the nature of our consciousness. Meaningful transformation could only occur from within. The sight we had witnessed was a powerful one—but no more so than the most mundane of scenes when viewed freshly by a mind truly open and present to its experience. It was time to return to our own culture.

Back in Alaska, we built a cabin on the shore of Kachemak Bay, where we lived for several years, maintaining as simple a life as we could and continuing our largely solitary practices. Yet, after a while, we began to experience another change we could not have predicted: we began to feel a certain arid quality to our lives, along with a growing impulse to come back into the world. We felt a yearning for more human contact, more interaction. We wanted somehow to take what we had learned in our years of solitude and apply it to the rich, messy vitality of "ordinary" life.

This impulse led us to leave Alaska—something we could not have conceived of just a few years earlier. It took us eventually to a village on the central coast of California, where we found like-minded people with whom we quickly connected. Eventually I trained there as a psychotherapist, while Martha developed a private practice of body and energy work. This time was also one of enormous personal challenge, for it brought us face to face with the difficulties of our own relationship—difficulties that our seemingly stress-free Alaskan lifestyle had allowed us to evade or ignore. We came to real crisis a few times in the hurly-burly of life in California; yet we managed to survive, largely through our conviction that relationship—our relationship—had become an essential part of our spiritual path. It was at this time that we first began working with couples.

The impulse to come more into the world also led us to become committed parents, an experience that for years I had resisted as somehow threatening to my spiritual growth, yet which has, in fact, taught me as much spiritually as any experience I have ever had. We had a son, whom we raised and home-schooled together, and who is now ready to start a family of his own. While we have not been exempt from any of the inconveniences of child-rearing, it has been altogether an unimaginable blessing.

Eventually our path led to rural Vermont, where we now do couples work as well as various other forms of counseling with a spiritual perspective. Though we give due priority to our inner lives, we live as householders, combining the earning of a living with quieter periods to meditate and to commune with each other and with nature. Our relationship is no longer something we need to isolate or protect from the world and its buffetings. Robust enough to survive the stresses placed upon it, our intimacy has ripened into a richness that feels as deep and fulfilling as anything in my experience.

A SUMMING UP

Today, I would say that my life as a husband, father, and householder has taught me as much about life as those first intense, quasi-monastic periods of solitude. The injunction to look within, rather than to circumstances, has never proved anything but reliable. But what the traditional teachings failed for the most part to convey was how fertile a field the life of a householder—especially one involved in intimate partnership—could be for revealing the contours of one's inner landscape. Everything I saw in my first glimpses of the Universe's one-ness has its application in the world of relationship, in the ups and downs of ordinary life, and in the exacting discipline of learning to open one's heart to another person.

This helps explain something slightly unusual in the pages that follow. This book is essentially about self-knowledge, about developing awareness of the inner landscape. Yet, in addition, considerable space is devoted to intimate relationship, to the task of applying awareness to our actual interactions with an intimate partner. At one level, of course, I stress this because it is the work I have chosen to do in the world; it is what I know. Yet this very work has led me to a conviction that relationship is the true frontier of spirituality. It is only in real life that the vision gained in solitude is put to the test. Intimate relationship brings us face to face with our most heavily conditioned habits of mind, the ones that breed our most powerful conflicts. What better territory for self-investigation? It was the acceptance of this challenge that led Martha and me, years ago, to commit ourselves to our own relationship, to bringing as much awareness and compassion as we could to our every interaction. And yet the impetus driving us was no different from the one behind our years of intensive meditation. It is the same impulse, the same longing for deeper satisfaction, that moved me to alter my life radically some forty years ago.

In reality, of course, the boundary between these two kinds of spiritual task—meditative and interpersonal, contemplative and active—is artificial. The fact is that self-knowledge has twin poles. One pole is the cultivation of pure awareness through meditation and self-examination. The other is what we learn from observing ourselves in relationship with the world. I try in this book to create a balance, a sense of equal importance between the two. Often the assumption has been that having spiritual insight made one automatically loving or wise, in total harmony with whatever arose in one's life. Once you had the vision, the ball game—so to speak—was over. But it seems profoundly true that such is not the case. We have only to look at the many cases of revered spiritual teachers coming to grief over issues like money, sex, and power to see the illusion of the "perfect" life for what it is. The reason for this, clearly, is that the conditioned entity holds far more power in daily life than meets the eye—more, even, than meets the mind in its quiet periods. One must get to know the conditioned self and its ways intimately, in its natural habitat (i.e., real life), before one can begin to deal with it wisely.

The spiritual journey ultimately unfolds in this pragmatic direction. My own progression from recluse to householder, from excited visionary to humbled realist, is not at all unusual. Many practitioners of meditation, particularly Westerners, tell of returning to the world after long stretches of monastic or contemplative life, periods in which they experienced moments of profound insight, only to find themselves wholly unequipped for the storms and tribulations of everyday life: a job, a relationship, a family. The inner peace they thought they had attained proved sustainable only in settings without disturbance; as soon as any kind of emotional turmoil arose, their equanimity was no greater than anyone else's—indeed, in many cases, less, because of their impossible expectations of themselves. For many of these seekers, as for me, the jolting return to ordinary life was the beginning of a long spiritual education, a process of learning to apply one's understanding to the messy complications of everyday existence. Apparently insight into the nature of things, in itself, is not enough; more needs to happen before it can be usefully employed toward a harmonious life.

It's not as though those periods of intense insight aren't of use. For me, the early years in Alaska were a time of awakening, highly important to subsequent ripening. My later experiences coming back into the world, first in California and later in Vermont, represented another significant branch of the tree, a branch more connected with opening the heart. As a self-described "recovering intellectual," one who had always been given to reflection (at times detached from my own feelings), I found that it was the branch I had the most to learn about. This helped me to appreciate that there were paths to self-realization other than the one I had initially chosen. Clarity of mind was not always the main thoroughfare.

There seem in fact to be two main kinds of spiritual path, both leading ultimately to the same place. One is wisdom, and the other is love: they are twin aspects of a single thing. Wisdom involves perceiving my true identity, looking deeply into my being to see that there are no grounds for fear at any level. And yet the natural state of consciousness without fear is a state of love. It took a while for this understanding to blossom in me. The "wisdom" part seemed to come more naturally when I was younger, while the "love" part, apparently, had to be developed through relationship. The path of clarity and the path of devotion are both amply represented in spiritual tradition; some connect more easily to the one, some to the other. At bottom, learning to be loving and learning to be wise are part of the same journey; both paths ultimately, inevitably, converge as one.

Returning, then, to the question posed at the outset: what does the application of spiritual insight to ordinary life look like? This question for me remains the crux of everything; it represents the essential substance of this book. Imperfection still remains my best teacher; anger, anxiety, sadness, frustration—all continue making their appearance, albeit less frequently. Confusions still sometimes stand in the way of clarity, and disturbances on occasion block the awareness of love. Yet I find that as time progresses, I can release my disturbed state more quickly and easily, returning to one in which clarity and compassion are at least possible. The road to Wisdom does not require us to eradicate the ego. The ego and its conditioning can be observed from a sufficient remove, from where one can smile at it. The space created by stepping away from the conditioned mind—this seemingly small separation—has helped immensely in allowing my heart to open. This may seem like a modest improvement, but it is remarkable how much this little bit of distance has expanded the fullness and satisfaction of life.

As I round the bend and enter my eighth decade, it has become much easier for me to feel the connection between loving and being deeply happy. In my moments of pure love, I experience a happiness that seems all-embracing—that is, not merely the opposite of sadness. Opening the heart can still at times be challenging, but, when I do it, I address any and all of my problems; indeed, every problem in the world I can think of would evaporate in the presence of love. This is why the book culminates with a chapter on Opening the Heart, and why I have come to see this task as the greatest of all spiritual challenges.

The readers I have especially tried to address in these pages are those who have experienced a certain level of discontent with their lives. Perhaps they have tried the usual means of achieving comfort, success, security, or happiness, and found them wanting. Perhaps they have begun to question their assumptions, to wonder if there is not another way, another purpose to life. If I had one wish for such readers, it would be to help them to see one fundamental thing: that all that stands in the way of happiness is the way the mind works; the only problem is "in here," not "out there," not in the way things are going, or in the way others are behaving. This is the great truth, and I believe it is well worth putting all one's intelligence and passion into its investigation.

When we embark on this spiritual journey, we do so with a vision of transcending fear and illusion, of attaining the freedom that is our birthright. Our vision takes form as we suspect, with growing personal evidence, that we have no identity as separate beings but are perfectly and harmoniously connected with all that is. Yet, as we pursue this vision, we encounter all the old demons from within the dream, the persistent illusion of being a small and solitary entity pitted against the threats of a vast, hostile universe. In encountering my own demons, my personal path has skirted a razor's edge. I have allowed my discontent to flourish, refusing to accept the conflict-making, heart-closing beliefs that have kept me locked in the limited prison of a confused mind. At the same time, I have honored the need of bringing to each moment a total acceptance of its content—including darkness and confusion. In the interplay between the "No" and the "Yes" lie the unexpected adventures of the Uncharted Journey. I walk through this life as both the dweller in Truth and the inhabitant of the dream. I have tried to speak in these pages from the creative tension between the two, acknowledging my humanness at all times, yet holding to the vision of freedom that beckons to us all.

I

DISCONTENT

Outside of infancy or occasional moments of joy, the majority of us seem more or less uncomfortable most of the time. Although I don't consciously think "There's something wrong with being here right now," I act as if it were the case. I support the notion through the persistence of my escape-oriented thinking and behavior. It is useful to inquire what is so wrong with this moment that it makes me wish to escape it.

When I become aware of my discomfort, I generally assign some particular explanation to it, usually having to do with my circumstances. Either something isn't going right in my life, or I fear that it won't in the future. But when I look more deeply, I see that, in addition to the specific discomfort of any given situation, there lurks underneath a more general uneasiness. This disquiet is so central to my being that it is elusive to normal awareness. At different times it manifests as anger, frustration, pain, hurt, anxiety, guilt, depression, or numbness. A sign of its existence is my inability or unwillingness to remain present in the moment. It is a cloud casting its shadow over all I do and think. It lies behind all I don't like about myself, my life, my relationships, and the world.

· · ·

From whence comes this essential discomfort? What's wrong with this moment that I find it so hard to remain in it? I could spend a lifetime escaping my discontent through the pursuit of pleasures, achievements, or worldly goods. None of it would resolve my soul's dilemma. Would not a saner option be to find the source of true comfort? It is my mind that creates this feeling of lack; the impact of my particular circumstances is infinitesimal compared to the mind's sway over my total experience. Would I not then be wiser and happier if I were to stop running away from my discomfort and instead apply my energy to transforming the mind that creates it?

~~~

A hallmark of our culture is its ubiquitous frenzy, arising from the almost universal discomfort in being with oneself. I interpret the flow of outer and inner events as either supporting my "self" or denying it. In the latter case, I feel the need to protect myself against the threat I have invented, and respond by tightening mind and body. Since this contraction invariably feels uncomfortable, I try to release the discomfort in a variety of ways. If I have the energy, I escape through pleasure, food, sex, drugs, relationship, business, art, politics, toys, sports, or trips. I distract myself with heady experiences, intense melodrama, beauty, fantasy, or entertainment. I also evade discomfort by planning for such distractions. Sometimes I escape through blaming others for my setbacks, justifying myself, denying my problems, or complaining. If my energy is low, I may escape through activities that numb me out and put me to sleep, such as mindless entertainment or various chemicals.

When my fundamental discomfort is great, the battle rages more forcefully between the "me" and the "not-me." All occurrences seem to lend the central discomfort a unique intensity; a business deal, a date, a sporting event can be dramatized or exaggerated beyond all proportion. The more attached I become to my escapes, the more I fear they won't relieve my distress. All my benighted attempts to address my distress serve further to increase it; this is one of life's classic vicious circles.

My intense and sustained frenzy keeps me doubly asleep. First, it supports the fiction that all this agitation will somehow lead me to an asylum of peace. Second, through frenetic activity I am emotionally numbed, postponing me from feeling and addressing the root of my fundamental sense of dissatisfaction. My mind keeps hoping that some new circumstance will bring at last that longed-for permanent state of undisturbed satisfaction. Removal from the present moment becomes a major theme of my life, exploiting the present moment as a mere stepping-stone to whisk me swiftly to the future, where I hope against all evidence that new experiences and pleasures will make my discomfort miraculously disappear. I fail to realize that when the future arrives, it bears little resemblance to the pleasurable state I had been anticipating. The same factors in the mind that cast their shadow on my current state will be just as operative, turning the hoped-for salvation into another unsatisfactory moment of Now. When that time arrives, I will again seek release through yet another future pleasure. And so on, ad infinitum. Even when good fortune occurs, instead of truly experiencing the satisfaction of the moment my mind races around, looking for ways to prolong my enjoyment or to make myself feel still better.

When I am uncomfortable, it is natural that I wish to find ease. Although the peace I seek does exist, it's not to be found in the future. It is not to be found in anyone or anything outside myself. Nothing has truly satisfied me, because the shadow currently cast by Fear will remain in each moment of Now. It will continue to do so as long as the fear has not been released at its core. If I am to find the comfort I seek, I need to respond now with a relaxation of my body, a quiet and spacious mind, an open and receptive heart.

⌒◯

When the truth feels unpleasant, my mind seeks to evade or hide from it. However, deeper investigation teaches me that the real Truth always feels good, and that discomfort arises only from illusion.

Whenever I ingest something toxic, Nature gives me notice to remove it. If I have been eating two foods, the first of which always gives me a terrible stomachache while the other results in my feeling healthy, light, and energized, it is not hard to conclude that the second is good for me and the first is not. If this applies to foods, why not attitudes, which are also a kind of food?

Nature signals my alignment or non-alignment with Truth by how I feel. Since the belief system upon which I have based most of my life until now has brought me much suffering, I might want to consider the possibility that my thinking is based on a false foundation. It could well be that the beliefs giving rise to my suffering bring pain because they are false. Discomfort may be present in order that I may locate, challenge, and release the toxic beliefs that create fear.

The value of fear lies in the very fact that it feels bad. Unless the feedback was uncomfortable, I would have no motive to investigate my deepest assumptions. But I can't make proper use of fear until I interpret correctly why my psychological toxicity feels bad.

As long as I see my discontent as something requiring me to control people and events, to seek more pleasures, to push against painful circumstances, I remain at its mercy. However, when rightly interpreted as the need to challenge the hidden assumptions behind my basic discomfort, the same discontent can be a powerful step toward freedom.

⁓

Is this fear at the core of my being founded on reality? This is an interesting question. Suppose I harbor a deep anxiety around money. It may seem to me that if I had a sufficiently large sum in the bank, I would have no more cause for fear. But is this true? A casual acquaintanceship with the lives of the wealthy suggests the answer. More likely, should I somehow attain the desired abundance, my fear would simply turn in other directions: I'll lose the money, or my wife or husband will stop loving me or die, or I'll get sick, and so on. Lurking at the end of it all is the specter of my death. The truth is, all my individual fears are simply hooks upon which to hang the elemental fear that is with me always.

What is the essence of this elemental fear? I suggest that the feeling of psychological threat is a false interpretation—the urge to protect gone awry. This urge is stimulated in turn by a belief: the belief that I am a finite, mortal entity, unconnected to the Whole of which the body is the symbol. The body will sooner or later stop supporting life, and what I believe myself to be, the ego, will utterly cease. I put symbols around the events in my daily life and—although the connection may be far from obvious—interpret them to signify that my being is continually threatened. It is this fear of non-being that haunts every lane and byway of my being.

Only that which is temporary can be annihilated; "danger" applies only to the world of form. The belief that I am form is the colossal mistake of the mind, which must be released to undo Fear at its source.

The tree of Fear has myriad branches; its trunk is this single intolerable prospect of not-being. I waste energy concerning myself with the shape of the branches instead of addressing the trunk. Although form is temporary, Being is eternal. The tree of Fear is uprooted through the understanding that my true nature lies beyond form.

I glibly assert my desire for "enlightenment," perhaps not realizing that it essentially means the ending of who I believe I am. The essential core of my fear is of the "me"—the being who is afraid—ceasing to be. In desiring enlightenment, I am in fact desiring that my biggest fear come true.

Are there many different problems, or just one problem variously manifested? Do I believe that my issues are different from others', or is there but one central dilemma for all human beings? When I reduce my problems to their essence, the only thing I see is Fear. As long as I embrace my primordial fear, I will never be at peace. The one problem has one solution, which is Love. In certain states of mind, I may find it difficult to find love. Instead, I look for a willingness to love or to trust. Seeing this simplifies my life immensely; when I am in a loving or peaceful state, my sense of having any problems evaporates.

~~~~⌒

I say I am afraid that something will happen. But if I look more closely I see that what I really fear is the disagreeable feeling that I suspect the circumstance will cause in me. If I imagine the most negative future situation, yet include the assurance that I can remain peaceful and happy in the midst of it, I cease to be afraid of it. All fear is ultimately of future uncomfortable mental states. Fear feeds on itself, fearing nothing but future fear. Contrary to the well-known maxim, however, I wish to challenge the notion that Fear itself is something to be feared.

Proceeding a step further, I realize that my fear of future unpleasant feelings arises from the belief that I will be unable to handle them. What happens to my fear if I experience the fortitude to deal courageously with whatever feeling may arise? Asserting my willingness to be uncomfortable, I feel a surge of strength, which immediately lessens my fear. This suggests that much of my fear is the unwillingness to be uncomfortable. If I have faith in my capacity to meet challenging moments with strength, Fear will cease to feel like a problem.

~~~~⌒

One part of me wants never to feel pain, hurt, or discomfort of any kind. The other part is willing to feel disturbance at the surface, knowing that being open to all feelings will bring me a deeper harmony. Being a warrior means dwelling in the latter place.

· · ·

My unwillingness to experience discomfort is frequently an avoidance of what I call "boredom," the true nature of which I fail to understand. Boredom requires first that I'm uncomfortable with my present reality because of my deep contraction. Next, I seek to escape the discomfort by finding something to occupy my consciousness: work, entertainment, computer, and so on. But I am unable to find a satisfactory distraction. Then I say I'm feeling bored. Much activity in our culture seems to be an avoidance of boredom, accomplished so efficiently that boredom is seldom actually experienced directly.

What is the actual experience of boredom? What does it feel like? When I allow myself to be bored, I see it as a "No" to what is. This moment is felt to be without value, except insofar as it can get me quickly to the next moment, where the mind believes my satisfaction lies. There may be value in allowing myself to experience boredom fully.

When anticipation loses its savor, I escape from the discomfort of Now by becoming tired or going numb. I am weary of struggling, unwilling to experience the fullness of darker feelings, so I "numb out" physically or emotionally. Such tiredness seems a precursor to illness and depression.

My discomfort has two levels: one is the actual feeling now in my body and being; the other arises from my resistance to the first. Resistance, the pushing against what is, prevents energy from flowing freely and leads to a more unpleasant quality of discomfort.

. . .

Awareness of resistance can end its effect. Consciously saying Yes to the totality of my experience in the moment helps to release unconscious resistance. I say Yes to my breath; Yes to my energy state, whether it's high or low, bright or dark; Yes to my current thoughts and feelings. Darkness passes more swiftly when embraced. My uncomfortable feelings are meant to be as temporary as an inhale or an exhale, but resistance turns the passing cloud into a long-dwelling fog.

Regret is resistance to the past, proclaiming "This shouldn't have been," rather than "What am I meant to learn from this?"

I am feeling extremely contracted. My pain and fear, my negative thoughts and feelings, my blame and self-loathing, my twisted perceptions, all feed on one another, ensuring their continuity. As I watch my pain indulge in this feeding frenzy, I stand in awe of its insanity. Everywhere I turn, my attention is smeared in black. The whole human race seems like a dismal, failed experiment, filled with such overwhelming suffering that I can hardly understand how anyone can get out of bed in the morning, or even to remain alive. I also feel immense blame and judgment for the endless stupidity so easily visible in every direction. I have nothing good to say about anyone or anything, especially myself. When my attention turns inward, I experience myself as even worse than what lies outside.

My challenge lies in seeing this contracted state as "it," not as "me." I observe it in action as a scientist observes a deadly animal seizing its prey, fascinated by the violence of it, yet unafraid. When I am able to succeed, it ceases to run me. My attitude is: Okay, Fear, I welcome even you. I'm going to shine a light on you and transmute you into something useful.

⟶

What is the interplay between discontent and acceptance? Both can be healthy expressions; both can be seized by fear and distorted. Divine Discontent, filtered through the distorting lens of fear, becomes resistance. Acceptance, seen through that same lens, turns into resignation. Yet when Fear is not in charge, discontent and acceptance do a graceful dance.

Divine Discontent is based on the natural desire to awaken from the dream of suffering. It comes out of a sense that a richer experience of life is possible and desirable. It is a flame without the smoke of resistance. The feeling of insufficiency is ego's version of Divine Discontent. They resemble each other in their dissatisfaction with the present. But the two are different in flavor: Insufficiency resists the present, reaching into the future for some experience that will eliminate present discomfort. Divine Discontent opens its arms to the present, while awaiting a spiritual opening in the Eternal Now.

⟶

Whenever I get upset, I support my belief that something can threaten or hurt me. Is the belief valid? Is psychological fear ever appropriate? Is my inner disturbance founded in truth? The answer to these supremely important questions will determine how I respond to discomfort in myself and others.

I see a coiled rope by the road at twilight, perceive it to be a poisonous snake, and react in fear. Upon closer examination, I realize that I was never in danger. Could it be that my whole life is lived in fear of a rope?

When fear arises, it is useful to take a searching look at the "snake" by investigating the belief that gives rise to the fear: I am unsafe when my partner speaks harshly to me; or I am unsafe when I don't get the job I sought. Here is a golden opportunity to make the highest use of skepticism.

If I'm feeling good, Fear whispers, "This won't last." When I'm feeling bad, it proclaims, "This is forever," contrary to all my previous experience. When have I ever been in a state that didn't change to something else? If, when I'm feeling depressed, I knew for certain that next Tuesday at 9:00 I'd feel fine again, the worst of my discomfort would evaporate right now.

                           ~∽

In the physical world, the principle of inertia asserts that a body in motion remains in motion unless acted on by an outside force. In the world of mind, fear tends to replicate itself, wanting to persist and flourish like a living being. To attain this end, it has developed a most convincing spokesman, an inner voice that speaks most persuasively. The Devil is a perfect symbol for this voice: attractive, compelling, logical. The voice of Fear entices with supreme cunning, offering me endlessly creative reasons why I should listen to its seductive voice.

                           ~∽

Amusement arcades used to have mechanical driving simulators with a red light that went on whenever the "car" left the "road." My consciousness has such a signal at its periphery. It glows whenever I lose touch with my core, or am not true to my nature. This automatic feedback mechanism is called suffering. I experience it as negative thoughts, contractions in the body, and the closing of the heart to what is, Now. It is a reminder that perhaps I need to seek another perspective. Unfortunately I get so used to the presence of the signal—somewhat like the stench in a chemical factory town—that it ceases to be of use to me. If I want to recognize swiftly when I lose my way, I need to regain my sensitivity to that signal.

As molecules of gas expand to fill the container, so a single fearful thought, left unchallenged, can expand into Fear's ultimate message: I am unsafe.

Fear commonly perpetuates itself through a classic vicious circle: the fundamental spasm at my ego's core gives forth negative, fear-based thoughts, which in turn intensify the deeper fear. A major step in breaking the circle occurs when those aberrant thought-forms, bubbling forth from the swamp of a confused mind, are no longer believed. Just as I needn't take seriously the ravings of a lunatic, I need pay no heed to my own mind's hysterical messages. Once I cease to believe in the fear-based thoughts, I can either dwell quietly in the darkness and let healing take place, or invite in thoughts that feel better. Both strategies are effective.

Attachment results from believing that something outside of myself can bring lasting happiness or safety. Such a belief invariably includes the fear of not getting what I wish for. My mind, misunderstanding the cause and the solution, falsely assumes that by controlling my outward environment I will be happy and free of fear. But since attachment is the origin of my fear, the only way I can truly free myself from fear is through releasing attachment.

A master of duplicity, Fear indulges in the charade of trying to get rid of itself through holding on tightly* to relationships, possessions, youth, or—ultimately—identity. Or it imagines a future pleasure and becomes attached to this new hope for relief, leading to fear that it will never come. The more tightly I hold on, the more afraid I am of loss.

Non-attachment can never be gained by forcefully superimposing spiritually correct principles onto my fear. That just drives it underground. Nor is there value in trying not to be attached. True non-attachment arises organically from awareness of my inner landscape. When I truly understand that all my efforts to control the transient and unpredictable outer world can never bring the peace I have been craving, those efforts are spontaneously released. The release occurs because I understand the deception behind all conceivable attachments.

I go to a place of intense beauty, such as the Grand Canyon, expecting to be so moved by its immensity and grandeur that my basic discontent will be relieved. To my chagrin, I discover that it doesn't work. A poignant contrast exists between how I believe the experience should make me feel, and my actual reality. Being in a beautiful place can actually increase my contraction when it disappoints in this way. The constant expectation that circumstances will relieve my basic discomfort leads me to an attachment-filled life.

·   ·   ·

Of course, I have a natural tendency to want to spend time in nice places, exercise and eat well, have good relationships and work that I enjoy. But there is a big difference when I reach toward these without the motive of escaping my fundamental distress. Once I no longer give circumstances the supreme importance of relieving my basic suffering, my life becomes oriented in a different direction. Without expectations, a part of my deep contraction is actually released. My preferences lose the quality of attachments; the future, no longer my salvation, ceases to hold such fascination.

My discomfort has two levels: one is circumstantial, the other is the deep contraction at my core, independent of circumstances. Winning the lottery, achieving a major success, falling in love, or encountering great beauty can temporarily reduce or eliminate the circumstantial discomfort. But no experience can touch the deeper level. This level isn't circumstantial, but rather arises from a belief that I am form, and can therefore be hurt, threatened, or cease to exist. The only complete solution to the deeper contraction is the realization that I am not form—otherwise known as "enlightenment."

While waiting for someone who is late in arriving, I realize that I have no need for them to be on time, or even to show up at all. When people don't show up or keep their agreements, they are merely being my current teacher in the ways of circumstance-free happiness.

Why does the traditional strategy, that of attempting to find happiness and security through controlling the external world, fail so completely? It's obvious that people and circumstances

can never be controlled. Yet I am attached to the world obey-
ing my will, living in constant fear that my attempt to control
won't work. I resent others for failing to be controlled, and I
end up feeling helpless. I fail to understand that it is my own
resistance and fear—rather than a failure to control—that prevent me from experiencing what I deeply want. Were I seeing
clearly, I'd be at peace in this situation; I would understand that
the change needing to occur is not in others. Even if I should
manage temporarily to control circumstances, I would never
find satisfaction at this level. The safety I have sought from
manipulating the outer world must be found within.

Releasing control is helpful if the attempt to control has arisen
out of fear. But there is another, more healthy kind of control:
the conscious choice of where I place my awareness. No matter what is happening, I have a say over how I greet this moment. I can choose to place my attention on either trust or fear.

Healthy control is the perfect balance for healthy surrender. The
first proclaims a lusty "no!" to what doesn't serve me on my
path. The second says "Yes" to the reality of this moment. The
first leads to self-mastery; the second to acceptance and peace.

⌒

There is value in cultivating choicelessness, wherein I seek to
respond in the same way to comfort and discomfort, acknowledging and accepting both equally. But it is also helpful to ask
myself: What are the assumptions that have given rise to my
discomfort? And are they true? To ask this is to shine a light
directly onto the shadowy belief that gives rise to fear: I am
not safe unless you approve of me, my child does well in
school, I have a certain amount in the bank, or my sex life

flourishes. Once I can articulate the belief that is causing discomfort, I ask myself: does this represent my deepest truth? The ego is extremely gullible; all of its assumptions, especially when they lead to discomfort, are worthy of divine skepticism.

One of my strangest beliefs is that I am not safe now, but that knowing the future will make me safe. This belief gives me reason to fear all that is unknown or ambiguous. Since this realm includes virtually everything, it assures that I should live constantly in fear.

Fear deals in symbols, and their acquisition is its royal road to safety. My discomfort increases in proportion to my emotional investment in the symbols I have assigned to keep me safe. If I believe I am safe because my business is doing well, my partner is faithful, my health is good—in short, if my safety depends on circumstances in any way—then I am already unsafe, because circumstances can and do alter beyond my control.

I have been trying to make myself safe by juggling symbols. I notice, of course, that it hasn't worked. What can be said of a "safety" that can vanish in a moment? Conditional safety isn't safety, any more than conditional love is love. All that arises from the premise of non-safety can only lead to non-safety. Whether this is felt to be a catastrophe or a great relief depends on whether or not I sense that there is an unconditional safety to be found in another dimension.

⌇

I say to myself that I'd like to be free of conflict. When would that be? If I locate my freedom in the future, I am creating conflict now, because I'm afraid the peace I wish for won't happen. In the Now, there is only this, that which simply is and has no opposite. Dwelling in the Now *is* freedom from conflict.

I imagine a great feast with superb dishes produced by the world's greatest cooks. I feel fortunate to be able to partake. Suddenly, seeing a fly on my plate, I become upset, and my enjoyment of the feast is spoiled. This is a parable of my life. In the main, I am healthy, I have great love in my life, I enjoy my work, I have lots of time to do what interests me, I have wonderful friends, I live in a beautiful place, I have a freedom that few cultures have enjoyed. Yet I can't be happy—or so I tell myself—because my car broke down, or someone insulted me, or I lost my wallet. Because my ego is attached to victimhood, I focus on the few negative factors in the midst of untold blessings.

Because I want to be at peace, conflict comes with a built-in desire for its own elimination. But why am I unable to eliminate conflict? It is because in reality, I am ambivalent about doing so. My desire to end conflict is simply more conscious than my opposing desire to continue the familiar (though painful) pattern of the known.

My attachment to the familiarity of conflict can remain elusive to the conscious mind. While feeling bad, I ask myself: if I could walk across the room and push a button that would bring me instant peace, would I do it? I notice a hesitation; I don't jump at the chance. If I follow my hesitation upstream, it leads me to my attachment to my current negative state. I am apt to complain, "I'm sick of this situation!" when in fact I'm only "kind of" sick of it, but also "kind of" attached to it. At some level, I may even enjoy it. The persistence of my complaining indicates that I prefer remaining in conflict to freedom.

Conflict endures because I have a reason for maintaining it. I may be addicted to it, derive meaning or passion from it, or fear releasing it because I associate it with my very identity. I tend to underestimate the tremendous hidden power of its centripetal force. My ego would rather retain the familiar suffering than risk entering the unknown.

In the midst of my misery, some momentary interruption makes me laugh. During the laughter, I'm admittedly not feeling bad. Then pain knocks on the door of my consciousness once more, as if it resents being displaced. Obediently, I return to the familiar negative feeling.

The same holds for depression: I believe I want to stop being depressed, but because it is as cozily familiar as an old pair of slippers, I have become attached to it. I offer weak rationalizations as to why I can't do something to make myself feel better. My fear of change is simply overpowering my distaste for suffering; yet I judge myself for this and call it laziness, or paralysis. In fact, I have merely failed to understand the natural consequence of my fear. When fear is released, the painful swing between anxiety and depression becomes the natural healthy alternation between passion and relaxation.

It helps to take my stand where I truly want to be. I can protect myself better and more efficiently when I'm not upset. I'm more likely to feel good about what happens when I'm at peace. I also tend to attract more favorable circumstances. I see that my deeper values are served at every level by following my wish to be at peace. To catch the mind in its addiction to pain is the beginning of freedom from the mechanism of suffering. When I am truly, unambiguously sick of conflict, I make an inner choice that frees me instantly.

I notice the presence of Fear. I feel where it lies in the body, experience its tightness, and breathe consciously with a soft belly. That already begins to change the way I feel, since breath and emotions are closely related and I am breathing more like one who is at ease. Softening around the fear as I would around a hypodermic needle, I consciously accept my fear as a momentary energetic experience. Rather than feeding its energy, I surround it with love.

Fear increases either when the mind accepts its premises and reasons from them, or when it fights against them. I don't do well treating Fear as a villain to be overcome. Rather I turn my focus away from fearful thoughts, giving them neither attention nor belief. When I am upset, I give myself room to be upset. I remind myself that I am feeling this way because of the way I am looking. There is another way of seeing the situation; I intend to allow it in. While accepting my present state, I ask for help in changing it. Because acceptance is now my reality, the mind relaxes and opens itself to the deeper dimension that heals.

Sometimes I am so caught up in negativity that I choose to stay closed even though I know the alternative is there. In such cases, it works best to give myself permission to retain my painful feeling as long as necessary. No matter what my momentary state, my natural rhythm opens me faster when I allow it to than when I fight against myself.

Asking "How do I get rid of my pain?" puts me in disagreeable conflict with my reality, only increasing my pain. If instead I inquire, "Can I find love in the presence of this?" it alters the nature of my quest. My reality becomes the love with which I surround the situation. The difficulty now assumes its proper proportion, a tiny piece of flotsam floating on through, rather than an overwhelming or immovable impediment to my well-being.

~

When do I wish to remain with a difficult feeling, and when is it wiser to turn away to something that feels better—perhaps a helpful spiritual perspective, or simply something pleasant? A subtle but important distinction exists between denying the feeling and challenging the belief that gives rise to it. Am I talking myself out of my feeling, or am I simply abandoning what I now see to be false?

Daily, garden-variety fear arises mostly out of habit. Thought slips into its well-worn groove, and the familiar discomfort appears. On such occasions, I may simply turn the dial to a different station by choosing a more peaceful thought, or by switching my attention to what feels better.

With more intense feelings, or ones that return obsessively, there is a greater possibility of self-delusion through employing spiritual perspectives to bury them. On the way to releasing the feeling, I may need first to allow myself to feel it fully, taking time to remain with it patiently and lovingly in order to receive its teaching. My deeper wisdom always knows when I have dwelt sufficiently in the darkness, at which time I turn my attention to the part of me that would rather feel love. Acknowledging that I am willing to feel good and don't know how, I open myself to an infusion of loving Truth from beyond my limited mind.

As a mother at a noisy gathering can hear the particular cry of her own child through the din, I learn to listen within for the initial impulse of fear. As I become better at recognizing it quickly, it has less opportunity to flood the mind. Only when I allow Fear to take root and grow does it become a challenge.

⸻

If I am to cease being a victim of my fear-based feelings, I need to stop identifying with them. Fear is simply an event in the mind; it happens. But when I identify with it, fear completely fills my inner screen, leaving no space for observation and investigation. To stop identifying with fear requires that I develop a capacity to witness it without being caught up in it. "I am so afraid!" is replaced with the gentler, more-allowing "Fear is present." To cease identifying is to shift the fear-driven engine from engaged to neutral. While still present, the feeling is no longer driving the transmission of my thoughts, feelings, and behavior.

I learn to develop my witness by lifting from the battlefield and perceiving with a smile the irrational and sometimes bizarre behavior of my inner mechanism. Without the witness, I *am* the mechanism. Once I cease to identify with it, I am no longer a prisoner of my history. Identification with a feeling gives it energy, while removing the sense of "I" deprives it of nourishment, allowing it to wither away.

Powerful emotions are hard to detach from; and developing the witness, especially around intense feelings, doesn't happen overnight. As I first learned to swim in calm rather than choppy waters, so I begin modestly with milder disturbances. Before I can unhook from rage, I must learn to put space around annoyance. For a time even this is challenging. Nevertheless, through regular practice with minor frustrations I strengthen a certain inner muscle that allows me to experience these upsets in a new way. In learning repeatedly to be a witness to my feelings, I prevent their running me. I thereby increase the intensity of emotional states from which I can unhook.

Meditation is especially valuable in this regard. Gradually, I learn to employ it, first in times of calm, then in the midst of minor upsets, and finally during moments of major unrest. One day I find myself able to stand back and observe even the most distressing emotions without being overwhelmed.

My initial goal may be to transcend ego-based feelings, hoping they will no longer arise. However, I soon find this to be an unrealistic expectation, since old pieces of negative conditioning have strong momentum and will likely continue to make an appearance for a while. Regarding these ancient feelings as unwanted guests in my consciousness is a form of resistance that serves only to increase their power. To cease identifying with such feelings is a more realistic goal than trying never to have them. When I cease to identify with a feeling, it loses power over me.

Fear resides in the body as well as in the mind. Everyone has a unique pattern of tightness in the musculature. The areas where I frequently tighten—diaphragm, vocal chords, facial muscles, shoulders, chest, stomach, neck, back, and so on—are accessible barometers that inform me unerringly whether I am responding to life with love or fear. I can gather useful information about my current state by checking in frequently with my body.

When I am a bit upset, in addition to softening the belly I may consciously adopt a subtle smile. Rather than being a denial of fear or pain, this gesture embraces it, like a kindly grandfather might regard his unhappy grandchild. By smiling at the uncomfortable content, I become the smile rather than the discomfort. The smile loosens the muscles in the face and can bring about an emotional softening. It expresses who I am in a more relaxed mode, less identified with my disturbing feelings.

Modern science is scarcely beginning to understand the connection between the inner landscape and physical pain. Illness, rather than some random and regrettable occurrence, can be a perfectly designed message from Me to me. Seeing illness as something that just happens to me implies that the body has its own life, independent of the mind. Perceiving the body as a servant of the mind may help free me from feeling like a victim. If illness is at some level a manifestation of fear, one of the best things I can do for my health is to greet my fear as lovingly as possible.

The mind sends out a directive to my whole being that it's safe to relax—or not. The signal traverses the body all the way to the cellular level, affecting my energy, mood, and health. It's good to be aware of which signal is being sent. Only then can I make a conscious choice to relax the cells and allow an infusion of healing energy.

⁓

I am walking on a beach in a howling storm, not enjoying myself. I come upon some seagulls, facing into the wind. I realize, in contrast to my own reaction, that they are perfectly content. The wind in some funny way is just blowing through them. They aren't resisting or complaining; they are saying Yes, completely present to what is going on. It strikes me that I have been saying No to the wind and rain, and also to much of my life.

While pain in its purity is an inevitable component of this dualistic life, suffering is the mind's unnecessary addition, arising only from resistance. I am programmed by thought and culture into saying No to pain, falsely believing that my resistance can protect me from it. Suffering is a call to understand the significance of this automatic "no," inviting me to find an alternative response to discomfort. Ego tries to convince me that I suffer because of people's behavior or some other external circumstance. In reality, I suffer from my failure to be more like those seagulls.

When I am feeling bad, I may safely assume there is another way of perceiving the situation, one that will at least end the suffering, if not the pain. I sense that if someone wise were placed in my circumstances, that person would remain at peace. But what is available to another is, after all, available to me too. In order to be receptive to it, I have to relax, become quiet, open my mind, and invite it in. In order to be open to a new perspective, I must be willing to release the old one. The elusiveness of Truth is directly proportional to attachment to the false.

By becoming intimately familiar with the pain-making mechanisms of my mind, I learn to release them. I learn about my own patterns of suffering by observing how others are creating theirs—and then recognize that I'm looking into a mirror. It is sometimes said that when I suffer, I must be choosing to feel bad. But I don't consciously choose to suffer. Nor is suffering being inflicted on me from without. What happens is that the ego fears choosing love—the choice that would actually feel good—believing it unsafe. I therefore choose a familiar belief or attitude that I mistakenly believe will keep me safe. This choice leads to my suffering.

Sometimes the flame of sadness burns with the smoke of self-pity, guilt, or blame. But if I refuse to push away my sorrow, deny it, complain about it, blame it on another, or make it into a soap opera, sadness can be held in silence and dignity, where its flame may be transmuted into compassion. Once suffering inspires compassion, it has served its function.

II

TOWARD
SELF-KNOWLEDGE

THE NATURE OF
CONSCIOUSNESS

Discomfort is an unavoidable part of my life. However, each moment of my discomfort can be experienced in a more positive way. If I resist when I'm uncomfortable, passively resign myself, or become angry and blaming, I miss out on an opportunity to make the inner shift that would cause me to feel better. The gesture by which this happens requires no preparation, psychological sophistication, or spiritual attainment. It is always available to me, independent of the content of my consciousness. It is simple, effortless, and feels good, as opposed to the ego's gestures, which are complicated and draining (they feel bad too, although the ego likes to think of it as the other way around). The only requirement is remembering to do it. The more I practice this inner gesture, the more often I remember it and the easier it becomes. One description for this fundamental spiritual gesture is letting go. Another is choosing love.

When I let go, what is it that I let go of? I release the need to control outer and inner experience, which means I am liberated from the controller, who in essence is the "me." Every day, I have the opportunity to let go of control, of needing to have my way. Daily practice with many little letting-go's gradually leads to an ease in letting go more deeply at the core.

There is no formula for being spiritual. Can "letting go" become a formula? Not really—not if it is truly letting go. My release of what brings suffering isn't a subtle attempt to attain; rather, it arises organically from understanding. I am holding on to something hot, pain is felt, and letting-go takes place.

In learning to relax and accept this moment, it helps to realize that I don't really know what's good or bad. I have only to look at the past to see this. I've so often been wrong—thinking something was "bad" when in retrospect it was merely a learning opportunity—that I no longer trust my judgment of what does or does not serve me. Without such judgment, letting go more easily arises.

⌒

Relaxation is a secular term, yet it lies at the heart of the ultimate spiritual gesture. Freedom and peace lurk in my parasympathetic nervous system.

When sleep-deprived or over-stressed, I may drift into an earlier pattern of feeling pressured, uptight, or reactive. I feel overwhelmed, believing there's too much to do, that I have to do it—and if I don't do it all, I'm in serious trouble. At such times, I forget that I can relax and allow it all to be done through me, the same way my breath takes care of itself nicely without my conscious effort or control. I'll do the best I can and release the rest. What more could I ask of myself?

·   ·   ·

"Thy will be done" is not the same as resignation, the ego's distortion of a deep truth; it is, rather, a total acceptance, in the moment, of discomfort or pain. I have faith that safety and peace await me on a deeper plane. I am willing to accept the current shape of the ocean's waves because I know that while the shape will change, the ocean abides eternally.

I see the value of surrender, but I am unable to accept certain aspects of my life that seem unacceptable: addiction, being overweight, the closing of my heart. Why should I surrender to the unacceptable? The conflict is resolved when I see how the unacceptable lives in time, while surrender is an inclusive acceptance of my life in this moment. In relaxing deeply into what is happening, whatever its content, resistance and fear are released. Now I am in a better position to act intelligently; my actions will no longer be reactive and fear-based. I accept my life now in order that its circumstances be open to change.

Ego, resistance, and fear are all aspects of one painful inner phenomenon, a great No to my experience. Saying Yes to this moment is an elegant way of stepping out. Every time I make this gesture of bringing my loving presence to this moment, it becomes easier for this eternally relevant neural pathway to reestablish itself.

An inner choice is possible in any moment of Now. Its beauty lies in its independence from the content of my experience. Honest examination quickly establishes that I can't directly control the content of my consciousness, as it unrolls moment by moment. But I can choose the way I greet the content. At bottom, there are only two choices: Yes and No. Yes is loving acceptance; No is fearful resistance. My conditioning instructs me to greet the pleasant content with Yes and the unpleasant with No. I have an interest in altering these instructions. In learning to choose the Yes as often as I can, especially in the midst of what is unpleasant, I bring a measure of grace to my life.

All uncomfortable feelings are remarkably similar, perhaps because they depend ultimately on resistance to what is. How much of the feeling of non-safety results from clinging to the pleasant and avoiding the unpleasant? I observe what happens to my fear when I consciously welcome all potential feelings. What then is there to be afraid of?

⁓

When I am so emotionally shut down that choosing love feels beyond me, I can perhaps locate my willingness to experience love. Even if most of me would rather keep a clamp on my heart, I may locate a small part of me that understands that being closed is living in Hell, and wants out. Dwelling here, I leave the window open for the breeze to blow in. I allow in the intention to experience love, the faith that it exists in me now, and the patience that knows it will arise at its proper time.

I slip on the ice, land uncomfortably, and have the wind knocked out of me. There is a moment's pause, and then . . . I burst unexpectedly into laughter. Looking back at my mental film, I see that just prior to the laughter was a moment of choosing either to get upset or to appreciate the ridiculousness of the situation. Even though I wasn't fully conscious of the choice at the time, by going over the film in slow motion I come upon that split-second of choosing to laugh.

I wish to develop this awareness more globally. The instant before I get upset invariably contains such a choice, usually unconscious. Only if I am aware at this key moment do I have what could really be called a conscious choice. If, after negative feelings, I rewind my inner film, observe the split second where I made my unconscious choice, and imagine making a different one, I increase the likelihood for such choice in a similar situation. Life will grant me many such opportunities.

⌒

Is the idea of a spiritual journey to bring about a perpetually "positive" state of mind in which I am always loving? Is spirituality a goal at which I either succeed or fail? If so, then whenever my experience is uncomfortable, I will judge myself to be spiritually inadequate and feel even worse. Better to redefine my spiritual task as the willingness to greet each moment with loving presence, and to forgive myself the rest.

The vocabulary for trust varies, although its essence remains constant. What is trusted can be described as God or some surrogate, depending on one's religious beliefs. But one can simply trust in a loving guidance from within, or that the Universe is safe, or that there's another way of looking, available now, which will bring peace. The particular symbol is irrelevant. The depth of trust is what matters.

Inside each of us, two teachers dwell side by side. They represent two basic thought systems: one the voice of Fear, the other of Loving Truth. Which voice I heed is my choice of the moment, and that choice, more than anything, determines how I feel.

.   .   .

I walk through a good part of my life believing unquestion-ingly in fear's assertion that the universe isn't safe. My fear gives rise to the strange belief that obsessing about how I might control the future will make me less unsafe. The strategy does not work. It places my safety in the hands of externals, rendering me a victim of a world I can't control.

I want to consciously choose the thought system in which I abide, rather than have it be chosen for me by my unconscious conditioning. I want to remember that my Loving Truth is always available. To make use of this wisdom I need to set my dial to receive its particular frequency. What help me are silence, pure longing, non-resistance, faith that help is available within, and willingness to receive.

Whenever I listen to my Deeper Wisdom, I have more energy, my behavior is more appropriate and helpful, my heart is more open, my thinking is clearer and more creative. With trust in the Whole, I can more easily relax and allow the parts to take care of themselves. Perhaps that is the only voice I should heed.

⌒

If I wish to challenge Fear successfully I need at least a mini-mum of faith or hope. In alchemy it used to be said that in order to make gold, one had to have a bit of gold at the be-ginning. The transmutation of base metals into gold represents the transforming of Ego into Loving Truth, a state without fear. If at the beginning I am willing to entertain the possibil-ity that I am now safe—my original measure of gold—I bring up this prospect to challenge Fear whenever it occurs.

· · ·

My fear can be gradually neutralized by persisting in my inner task of challenging my beliefs. Even if it feels as though fear is ninety-eight percent and trust is two percent, I have the option each moment of choosing to find the two percent and put my attention there. Wherever I regularly put my attention gets strengthened. Over time, the two percent grows, eroding my belief in the false. I become more relaxed and open, so Truth can penetrate my defenses. Over time, my fear becomes more subtle, transparent, and inconsequential. This patient inner work transforms a modest suspicion of safety into a deeper faith.

The ego has its own version of trust. It consists of Fear's unsuccessful attempt to get rid of itself. Starting with the premise that I am not now safe but can become so, I hope for something outside of myself that I can "trust" to make me happy or secure. I base my sense of safety on a particular out-come: that a certain person will continue to love me, that I will stay healthy, or that the economy will remain sound. But whatever initiates from a premise of fear can never result in feeling safe. Even if hoped-for events transpire, there's no way they will ever bring the desired safety. I can't *become* safe; I can only know that I *am* safe. This level of trust is sometimes called faith; it exists beyond the world of form and is not dependent on events to sustain it.

When I think of faith as belief without any substantial reason, the idea has no resonance for me. But when I look within, I do find intimate evidence that faith is warranted. This evidence originates from moments of experiencing an asylum of peace, independent of externals. With attention to itself, it increases. I have faith in a transformation of consciousness, in my ability to become aware that I dwell in eternal safety.

· · ·

Trust and Fear live in me side by side, with either available as a choice in the moment. Fear has been my default setting, the place where I go when I'm unconscious. The biggest factor in undoing the default setting is learning to be conscious. My chief aid in learning to choose trust more often is simply remembering that it's an option.

A slogan on a bus: "Leave the driving to us." I imagine settling back into a soft, comfortable seat, letting my nervous system unwind, and watching the world go by, releasing all need to do anything. The words could be a statement of my own faith.

My powerful longing to arrive Home arises from the deep sense that there is such a place. Although my intellect can make a logical case for its reality, it can also assert with equal logic that the concept of an Asylum of Peace is nonsense. If I am so inclined, I can find much to be cynical about in the world. Although both thought systems are logical, the intellect is out of its depth in this realm. The truth must come from another dimension.

Is it possible to awaken from the dream of being an ego in constant danger? We hear of great spiritual figures who seem to have done so. Why should I assume it's possible for them but not for me? They were human beings like me, who found freedom because they took their stand by applying themselves to spiritual questions with great passion. If I am willing to do that too, can't I find the same answers? Can't anyone?

I fear not being able to take care of myself when I am old. But the real issue is not whether I can take care of myself; it is whether I believe the Universe will take care of me. How could I claim to have faith if I believe I've got to do it all myself?

I have a choice in each moment: whether to place my consciousness in my faith or my fear. When I try on the notion that the Universe will take care of me, my whole being relaxes and feels energized. By how I feel, I can tell which of the two beliefs I am embracing.

⌇

The great teachings tell me that all is well as it is; nothing in my experience needs to change. Yet the feeling that "all is well" is elusive; it would seem that something needs to change in order for me to experience my life in peace and harmony. Perhaps what needs to change is not the content of my experience, but rather the way I interpret it. Everything I experience is seen through a particular interpretive filter, although I believe what I see to be reality. When I fail to examine my interpretation, I lose sight of the fact that it represents merely one among several possible ways of seeing the situation. My normal perceptions are limited and pain-producing—good reason to explore whether there is an alternative to them.

My partner or a friend criticizes me, I falsely interpret that as danger, and feel hurt or angry. My discomfort is then further interpreted: How blameworthy or justified am I for having the reaction? What is its significance, its effect on others, its justification, its origins in the distant past, and so on? I might do better to investigate the true source of my discomfort. If my interpretation of events were to vanish for just an instant, what would happen to my discomfort?

· · ·

The spiritual journey is undertaken so I may understand that my present interpretive filter is optional. I have a simple feedback mechanism that unfailingly lets me know when my interpretation is untrue: I feel bad. Normally I misinterpret the reason for this as well, thinking it to be caused by others or by events. I try to get rid of the feeling by controlling people and circumstances, always unsuccessfully. I am better off to perceive my discomfort as arising from the toxin of false interpretation. Every unpleasant feeling has a false thought lurking somewhere behind it, shoring it up. My task is to discover that thought and challenge it. Discomfort is a call from the Universe to investigate, to find a truer picture of reality.

I drink a glass of white liquid, thinking it is milk. Expecting the familiar taste, I recoil with disgust at the jolt of unexpected sourness, spitting it out violently. I see that the liquid was actually buttermilk and arrive at the clear, unequivocal conclusion: I hate buttermilk. I vow that I will never let such dreadful stuff pass again through these lips and persist in this attitude for years. Meanwhile, I come to like yogurt very much. Two different foods, no contradiction. Then one day it occurs to me, yogurt is sour; isn't buttermilk a kind of liquid yogurt? I then try some buttermilk, and in this context find it delightful.

I sense that most of the negative flavor in my experience, originally imputed to the experience itself, arises instead from my resistance to that experience. There are many examples of "buttermilk" in my life. They suggest my capacity to transform an experience from uncomfortable to comfortable through a shift of perspective. The balm of awareness softens the need to resist.

• • •

Applying the same principle to emotions has important spiritual implications. If I choose to view another's unloving behavior as a fearful cry for help, instead of a threatening insult to my pride, I release the unpleasant feeling of a closed heart. The facts are the same; I merely change the context. The energy that goes into trying to control the outer world is better spent in exploring how to change my interpretation. This, more than anything else, will determine the quality of my experience.

When a situation feels stuck, what needs to become unstuck is attitude. That it is possible to alter my attitude is beyond dispute. There are those who have been happier and more at peace in a concentration camp than others living lives of supreme comfort.

As long as I carry false beliefs, I will attract people and circumstances that challenge me. This helps keep me honest. I may arrange a life in the wilderness where I am undisturbed by outside forces. Yet my "peace of mind," superficial and brittle, may only encourage me to retain my false beliefs. When I enter into a more normal life, the disturbance may be shocking. Yet this can be a true blessing; it helps me release my belief that feeling comfortable is good and feeling uncomfortable is bad.

When I awaken from a dream, I can easily grasp the fact that I wrote the script and created the whole show. Every character was a part of me in disguise. A bit more elusive is the understanding that in my waking dream, the same thing is true.

· · ·

I can imagine my life as a multisensory attraction in an amusement park of the future. I could step into a booth, choose from
a variety of possible lives, plug in, and, in a few minutes, experience the drama of an entire lifetime. The drama becomes
intensified because I forget all is well. Perhaps I am at this
moment in such a booth.

Everybody wears a costume, attractive in varying degrees to
others in appearance and personality. Being on a spiritual journey doesn't mean getting rid of the costume; it does mean
relating to it differently. In performing this role that I call "me,"
I tend, when unaware, to become totally identified with it. An
inner switch is possible where, instead of *being* the role, I experience myself more as the actor *playing* the role. Suddenly I
am less caught up in life's drama. As the actor, I relish playing
the role well without taking it too seriously. Identifying with
the trivial aspects of my costume keeps me from seeing my
beauty. When I see something I don't like about myself, it eases
my burden to regard it as part of the costume.

I understand at the deepest level, the costume is illusion, not
who I am. I can nevertheless gaze lovingly at the figure I think
of as "me," with all its peculiar characteristics. When those
traits are expressed consciously, my life is more agreeable.

The fervor of life's drama is not necessarily a function of the
actual intensity of life, but rather of the way its events are
regarded. Drama arises when the dream's fluctuations are
treated as momentous and taken seriously. In understanding
the inner landscape, the dream becomes more transparent, the

play of light and dark less serious. I still prefer to be healthy, but I am not so identified with or attached to my preference. Because my fear loses its urgency, the drama subsides; I can relax and enjoy the show with a bit more grace and humor.

Ego loves to play at being spiritual. Being on a spiritual path, I tend to be as judgmental as anyone else, feeling superior with a "spiritual" flavor. Indeed, the ego has its own version of every spiritual quality:

- Indifference is the ego's version of equanimity.
- Pity is the ego's version of compassion.
- Walking on eggshells is the ego's version of sensitivity.
- Pleasure is the ego's version of joy.
- Instant gratification is the ego's version of living in the Now.
- Grandiosity is the ego's version of self-love.
- Pride is also the ego's version of self-love.
- Resignation is the ego's version of acceptance.
- Resistance is the ego's version of Divine Discontent.
- Expectation is the ego's version of intention.
- Guilt is the ego's version of remorse.
- Self-judgment is the ego's version of self-awareness.
- False modesty is the ego's version of humility.
- Impatience is the ego's version of the soul's longing.
- Sacrifice is the ego's version of giving.
- A truce is the ego's version of harmony.
- Melodrama is the ego's version of passion.
- Complacency is the ego's version of peace.
- Attachment, neediness, infatuation, and lust are the ego's versions of love.

Compassion, Love's response to suffering, is often conceived as the need to join someone in their pain. Ego asserts that if I don't respond by feeling bad myself, then I'm not really compassionate. It is considered compassionate to show concern for someone who is sick or feeling bad. But I notice how suspicious and uncomfortable it can feel if I'm feeling ill or down and someone enters my world acting or seeming to be "concerned" about me. Concern, when polluted with fear, may convey the sense that I lack the capacity to learn from whatever lesson the Universe is presenting me. It implies that there is something wrong with the fact that I am in this state, that I am in danger.

In an unsafe world, suffering is the proof of lack of safety—mine or another's. In a safe world, Love perceives no danger. It sees the other as merely caught in a bad dream of suffering, from which they can gently wake up.

When someone is at ease in the presence of my discomfort, it conveys to me a sense of safety. This empowers me to deal with the situation; I feel blessed and healed by such a presence. I wish to offer the same to any other. Instead of joining in their suffering, I can help them best by showing them my love, wishing them well, letting them know they are safe, and making myself available to help them alter their perspective if appropriate.

The path of self-knowledge yields its fruits increasingly as I learn to become more comfortable with my discomfort. This allows me to study my inner landscape in depth at close range.

Slowing down my inner film, I make many observations; I then connect them with other observations until patterns emerge. It starts with a few faint, unconnected clusters that gradually take on more clarity and detail, like a developing Polaroid picture. Ultimately, they connect to one another to form a coherent whole.

Investigating the way Fear plays itself out helps me avoid getting caught up in it. A botanist goes out into the field and recognizes previously described plants. I benefit from investigating different species of the family called Fear and developing sensitivity to their nuances. As I come to know them better, they are more easily recognized and released. Not getting caught in fear frees me to be present for my life as it is unfolding. Being present for my life allows me to see beyond the limited structures of mind, into my true identity.

Moving toward self-knowledge requires no highly developed intellect, no psychological sophistication, no metaphysical or spiritual acumen. It works on a simple principle: whenever I feel good at my core, I am closer to Truth.

⌒

Gold has a certain essence, independent of the objects crafted from it, which can be melted down and made into other objects. I likewise have a "golden" essence. It can be formed by the mind into all kinds of shapes, but none of them affects the essential nature of my being.

One of the shapes created by the mind is Ego. Love, in its purity, gets filtered through a thoroughly distorted belief system, emerging in my conscious mind as a seemingly unloving state. Ego, contemplating itself, fails to appreciate its golden essence, seeing only something worthless that needs to be masked or destroyed.

The world of the many is filled with the good and bad, ugly and beautiful. I want to remember the perspective of the One, which knows my true nature as gold, an essence whose form, however temporarily distasteful, is supremely irrelevant.

~⌒⌐

I look back on my life and see two stages. In the first, the Great Inhale, I take in many experiences, giving importance to the form my life takes. Exuberance and passion are present, although I may at times give form so much importance that I get attached, and then fear its loss. My natural ripening can lead to a Great Exhale in the later stage of life. Here I learn to release attachment to form, and, to the extent that I succeed, attain greater peace. These years feel like a natural time for releasing my ultimate attachment to form: the body, its possessions, its status, and ultimately its identity.

As one grows older, the valleys are exalted and the hills made low. Although some sensory impressions remain more pleasant and others less so, the particular quality of experience seems to matter less; I feel decreasing desire for new experiences. My attachment to beauty and sensual gratification as potential removers of pain evaporates, giving way to a quieter appreciation of all that is. The quality of my life arises increasingly from whether or not my heart is open, and little else.

.   .   .

Contained in the very nature of my discomfort is my wish to rid myself of it. No matter what I am suffering, my mind will always have plans for becoming more comfortable. The nature of these plans is based on my level of understanding. If that level is low, the plan will be to bring about and retain certain pleasures, preferably uninterrupted. Greater understanding produces the desire to bring about a future transformation of the mind itself. With still greater understanding comes the knowledge that this transformation is always Now.

Different cells in a leaf can be seen as aspects of the same leaf. To a cell, another cell need not be "other"; nor, to each other, are the different leaves of a tree. My notion of "other" people depends on my failure to see that I am in essence part of a single "organism." This sense of being unconnected is the source of my painful illusion.

As the cell is part of the leaf, the leaf part of the tree, and the tree part of the forest, so I am a part of something greater. When the cell dies, the leaf, the tree, and the forest don't consider it a tragedy. It's only a "tragedy" when looked upon from a limited perspective. Am I a mere cell? Moments of awakening have shown me I am part of Something that could never be threatened or hurt.

Encountering so many spiritual perspectives, how do I determine which ones to take seriously? One of the better criteria is what feelings about myself they trigger. Any notion that encourages me to feel bad about myself, I suspect as coming from Ego. The Source of All Being has got to be at least as kindly disposed toward what seem like imperfections as a good mother.

What will I employ as my authority for Truth? My fickle intellect, with its capacity to wrap itself around whatever Ego finds attractive? This has proven quite unreliable. What others assert feels even less satisfactory. If the notion of authority has a legitimate meaning for me, I would say Love has its own unmistakable stamp of Truth. Only my heart truly knows.

A heady enthusiasm accompanies the first stages of my spiritual journey, as new insights tumble rapidly over one another, seeming to produce rapid transformation and even exalting experiences. There is an anticipatory excitement, as Ego senses in the near distance the ultimate spiritual triumph: its own death—with itself grandly giving the funeral oration. For a short time I retain the belief that my new spiritual perspective is going to bring me uninterrupted happiness. This is followed by gradual disillusionment, as I realize that permanent satisfaction isn't arriving on schedule. At this point, Ego complains: "I don't seem to be making much spiritual progress. Once again, I am a failure."

What slows down my spiritual transformation is the heavy conditioning of my core issues, which require patience to even identify, let alone transform. Some areas of life may quickly become more harmonious, but others will stubbornly resist change. A deeply ingrained pattern of behavior, for example, or the residue of a relationship with a parent, may retain many of its tiresome patterns for a long time before softening. To expect universally swift growth is like a beginning runner hoping immediately to complete a marathon. As in learning a musical instrument or a language, I need time to prepare myself. Inner work requires strengthening, accomplished patiently with the tools at my disposal: meditation, honest self-observation in my relationship with others, and a constant exploration of fresh ways to let go of the mind's habitual attachments.

In the early stages of self-awareness, I experience frequent bursts of shame as I become rapidly aware of my unconsciousness and self-centeredness. The more I observe my ego in action, the more my image of myself as a "nice" person is shattered. This painful stage subsides only when I begin to suspect that this distasteful ego is not my true identity.

I catch myself being unaware and, instead of being grateful that I caught it, I judge myself for not living up to my spiritual ideals. My ego scolds, "How will you ever become spiritual if you spend so much time being unaware?" This is another case of Ego donning a spiritual costume. It gives itself away by employing violence as a means toward loving peace.

⁓

Forgetting to be aware is not a "problem." It is in fact merely a reminder to be more aware. Whenever I blame myself for falling into old mechanical behaviors I assert that my path should progress in a straight line, without any backsliding. It is difficult to find straight lines in nature. Like evolution everywhere, mine occurs in fits and starts, as moments of forgetting are interspersed with moments of remembering. It is all part of life's naturally alternating rhythms: pleasure/pain, light/dark, summer/winter, remembering/forgetting.

. . .

Acknowledging to myself the inevitability of forgetting, I release the obligation to be a saint who remembers all the time. Such impossible goals lead to frustration and self-castigation. Fretting about forgetting, making it "bad," or obsessing about how I can forget less, is to indulge in another level of forgetting. The same is true of the fear that I will forget in the future, or fail to remember all the time. What interests me instead is remembering Now, for that's something I can do. Substituting "Now" for "all the time" aligns me with Truth.

Forgetting provides its own feedback mechanism, invariably some form of discomfort. I can interpret my loss of peace as a call to recognize that I have fallen asleep. It doesn't matter how long my unconsciousness has lasted; at the moment of its discovery, it ceases to be. The very recognition that I have been forgetting *is* remembering.

Over time, my remembering feeds itself and becomes stronger, while the forgetting becomes less frequent, less intense, and shorter-lasting. Releasing the pressure to remember leads to a relaxation that ultimately encourages more remembering.

To live with awareness can be arduous. Sometimes in moments of frustration I may wonder about the point of so much focus on awareness. But in asking "What's the point?" I am embracing the traditional goal-oriented view of a spiritual path—that leads from one place to a "better" one. The mind complains of laboring at this seemingly burdensome spiritual task, fearful that its toil won't yield the hoped-for salvation.

. . .

In truth, the "point" is found only in the moment. I have a choice to live each moment aware or unaware. I would rather do it with awareness, not because of some future gain, but because of the inherently more interesting quality of my life when I am present for it. I know in my bones that I would rather be conscious than unconscious. I know that I would prefer to experience my life without a distorting filter.

One way of defining true intelligence is the capacity of my mind to be consciously aware of what I deeply want, and to serve me well by helping me to give my best in obtaining it.

Self-centeredness, stripped of its ignorance, is an attitude that asserts, most reasonably, "I deserve love." Instead of fighting against something so natural, I can make it broader and wiser. A narrowly self-centered person who finally realizes that his life would be happier if he were kinder to those around him still cares about his own well-being, although he now sees its connection to the well-being of others. Ultimately, self-centeredness is Life loving itself; the distinction between Self and Other vanishes.

My inner work teaches me to recognize four stages of ego:

1. Unconscious indulgence of Ego. This is the state I am in before I awaken to the presence of Ego lurking behind all of my suffering.
2. Seeing Ego as the enemy and trying to overcome it. This stage occurs when I recognize Ego as the source of my problems, but don't as yet understand that fighting against myself is but another manifestation of Ego.

3. Consciously observing and allowing Ego without taking it seriously. This is the stage of an awakening mind, in which I penetrate the complexity of Ego's tricks. Recognizing the fallacy of making Ego into an enemy, I realize that awareness of Ego is sufficient to step out of it.

4. Knowing Ego as unreal. The ultimate goal of the spiritual journey is to experience my identity within all of Life. Finally there is a direct understanding that the separate self, a product of a confused mind, has no existence.

⌒

The natural surface-level fluctuations of my consciousness, responding to my body's chemistry and to the events of my daily life, will always be with me. However, they take place against a deeper background that is usually unconscious. If the background is fearful, the downturns feel terrible while the high spots remain unfulfilling; I'm always leaning into the future, looking for greater pleasure. If the background is love, safety, peace, the good moments are deeply satisfying and the downs superficial. My feelings become lighter when I allow the surface to be what it is and attend instead to the background. The latter, through self-knowledge, relaxes and harmonizes over time.

⌒

Am I here for myself, or for others? The answer may be: is there a difference? Whatever talents I have will best serve the world if I am at peace, happy, loving, free of fear. What serves my deepest well-being answers as well to the highest good for the world; in caring for the world, I honor myself. Generosity toward the world and toward myself ultimately coincide.

.   .   .

A good way to measure what I am putting out in the world is
to be aware of the way I talk about those with whom I disagree. With every interaction I either increase the general fear
level in the world or decrease it. When the message I convey is
that there are things to be hated and feared, I am hardly
advancing the cause of peace. My legacy to the world could be
summarized by whether or not my presence here has allowed
others to feel more safe than before.

~———

The notion of "better" and "worse" is a breeding ground for
paradox in the spiritual world, because we live simultaneously
in two levels that tend to get confused. The level of the many
is our daily life, the world of preference, of dualism. Living in
this world, I've got to be dead not to feel that some things are
preferable to others. If I deny preference, I am asserting that it
is all the same to me whether my child becomes a happy, successful person or a drug addict. If I have suffered, how can I
not wish suffering to end? How can I not wish for love and
peace, in my heart, in my relationships, and in the world? How
can I not believe that it matters?

When I look to traditional religion, it seems to tell me that it
does matter. It teaches me that it is better to be good, loving,
kind, forgiving. The difficulty arises when I dwell solely in the
world where this is preferable to that. My perfectly valid preference becomes laced with attachment, the fear that what is
desired won't happen. I tend to look at ugliness and violence
as ultimately bad and regrettable, something to be fought
against. A defining struggle between Good and Evil is the outcome. I come to look upon others who disagree with me
as the enemy, furthering strife and ill will. I become so

ensconced in my fear of losing the battle that I fail to enjoy my
life as it is happening. My state of resistance keeps me from
attracting what I want.

When something really matters, there is passion, which gives
meaning to life. Yet as it is normally experienced, passion has
an anxious quality. If I make some perfectly natural preference
into an absolute, then I come to believe that I require it in
order to feel good. This gives me reason to fear that what I
passionately want won't happen. Passion, uninformed with
wisdom, sees every situation as absolutely desirable or regrettable. God isn't in His/Her heaven unless events unfold to my
liking.

An understanding of non-dualism, by adding another dimension of Truth, helps to counteract this difficulty. This world is
seen to be a dream, a place of illusion, in contrast to the world
of the One (or God, or Cosmic Consciousness). Because the
particular shape of our illusions doesn't affect what is real, all
manifestations are seen as fundamentally equal. From this
outlook, secure in the knowledge of divine safety, I can adopt
an attitude of choicelessness, an equanimity toward all events.
Undisturbed by the changing tides of fortune, I am freed from
a deeper level of fear. This allows me to do more "good" in this
dualistic world.

But does this mean that it doesn't matter? Non-dualistic
teachings, in attempting to release attachment, sometimes
seem to deny the legitimacy of preference. As the Fifth Patri-
arch of the Zen tradition says, "The perfect way knows no difficulty, except that it avoids all preference." Yet a lack of

preference can lead to a lack of passion. What is there to be passionate about if it's all the same to me? Without passion, where is my life's meaning?

I cannot deal effectively with my fear through numbness or indifference. If I try to, non-dualism may attract me for the wrong reason. Trying to convince myself that it doesn't matter, I am drawn to a spiritual perspective that supports this. I may lower my conscious fear level (though probably not my deeper layers), but the price I pay is the sacrifice of passion. I have confused equanimity with indifference.

Rather than trying unrealistically to overcome preference, I may find that it makes more sense to purify the flame of preference from the smoke of attachment. This frees me from guilt over the perfectly natural fact that I find some things more desirable than others. Non-dualism needn't be interpreted to mean that nothing matters. I may take seriously whatever I wish, but I consider that the fear surrounding my passion may be based on a misperception worth exploring. With a major part of my consciousness ensconced in non-duality, I carry the knowledge that at bottom it's just a play, that I'm safe and the world is safe. My non-dualistic understanding is a ground upon which the dualism of my nature plays itself out. It provides a loving embrace to all my struggles, softening the finality of my prison as I await my freedom.

Spiritual wisdom exists in proportion to how well one integrates the two attitudes: it matters and it doesn't matter, dualism and non-dualism. Because it matters, there is passion; because it doesn't matter, there is freedom from fear.

· · ·

The dualistic perspective supports "better" thoughts; the non-dualistic perspective encourages no thoughts.

Are there exceptions to spiritual truths? Fear proclaims "All this spiritual stuff may be okay for trivial matters, but when it comes to the really important issues—marriages, jobs, large sums of money—that stuff doesn't really work. I am master there, and I need to be hard-headed." Do I believe this, deep down? Am I keeping the back door of my spirituality open so I can escape when things get tough?

Fear may also say "I believe in being loving in general, but not toward *that*." As long as I hold on to being resentful toward anyone or anything, I demonstrate my disbelief in the spiritual truth I claim to embrace: that it all deserves love. The being I have the greatest trouble forgiving, my "Holy Nemesis," may be the one who shows me most clearly where I still hold back.

I enjoy contemplating and applying spiritual truths except insofar as they pertain to where I am most ill at ease. To the extent that I believe these truths have exceptions, I don't understand them. By their very nature, spiritual truths can have no exceptions. Either I can be threatened or I can't. If I can sometimes be threatened, then I am never really safe.

I wish to apply my deepest insights to the most difficult areas in my life, because that's where they prove their reality. Whenever I have a seemingly spiritual insight, I train myself to apply it immediately to my arena of greatest fear. If I don't feel instantly better, I haven't really seen anything.

Two words I feel a vague discomfort in using are "God" and "love," because of the meanings they have accumulated through the years. The former implies a being out there, separate from who I am, at best loving me only if I deserve it. The latter connotes something that needs to be earned through good behavior. In the presence of such intuitively false connotations, Truth cries out for an alternative vocabulary.

One hesitates even to use the word "evil," especially to apply it to others. It implies that that the recipient of the epithet doesn't deserve love. This puts me in the position of playing God, deciding who does and doesn't deserve love—a slippery slope upon which I don't care to step.

To posit the existence of evil suggests something real that must be fought against. With this stance, Ego is on familiar ground, one of opposing and excluding. A duality between Good and Evil is asserted, placing them on the same plane. Evil is perceived to be just as real as Good, therefore a dangerous force against which one must do battle. The ego's version of spirituality says I must devote myself to battling on the side of Good in the hope that it will ultimately triumph in the struggle. In this war, whose outcome is never certain, there is no relaxing; I am eternally unsafe. A teaching that talks of fighting against Evil is one that has been usurped by Ego.

If Truth feels good, does this disturbed and decidedly un-peaceful outlook not suggest the possibility of a different and truer way of seeing? Could it be that the duality of Truth and illusion is only apparent, because they are not actually on the same plane? Perhaps "Evil" has but the reality of a nightmare or a shadow. Perhaps there never was any threat, and my whole perception of danger is an illusion.

Whenever I oppose something in myself, I assert its reality, granting it additional strength through the frequency of my attention. What isn't real requires no opposition. For the same reason, there is no need to give it energy by analyzing it, discovering its roots in the past, or taking it seriously in any way. Perhaps I would do better to turn my attention to what is real. In truth perfectly safe, I nonetheless dream I am in danger; to escape, I must only awaken. In moments of Truth, absolute safety is my most powerful experience. It makes intellectual sense, it makes emotional sense, it makes spiritual sense. In the absence of total faith, I act as if this approach is true, and then observe its effects: I feel more at ease, more peaceful, happier, lighter. Is there a better barometer of Truth?

As an expression of the world's seeming duality, perhaps Love and Fear makes more sense than Good and Evil. It is a different relationship, since Love, instead of trying to overcome Fear, embraces it.

Can one experience "evil" directly? I become deeply caught up in a violent rage, feeling myself to be a "devil," having a supreme tantrum from the center of the universe, spewing ruination on all of creation. The being I have become would annihilate the universe if it could. The awfulness of it, the ugliness, the immorality! And, as Ego, how gleefully I embrace it. There is something perversely satisfying in this universal hate. It is at bottom how the beast within, stripped of its "reasonable" mask, regards whatever it considers the "enemy."

. . .

Perhaps such an experience can help me understand an "evil" that seems otherwise beyond comprehension. A mad dictator, frustrated by a defeat, decides in a rage to burn a historic enemy city to the ground. Is such an act beyond my comprehension? The dictator's ego may express itself on a vast scale; but is it different in essence, in quality of mind, from my own wish to annihilate what is perceived as the not-self, the enemy? Even the ego's most destructive attitude toward the enemy can be traced ultimately to a loving motivation, however twisted. The mother tiger, out of protective love for her cubs, kills an animal—the not-self—that approaches this extension of her self too closely.

The quantity or scope of Fear's expression is not a measure of its immorality; goodness and its opposite are not defined by scale.

When I create out of love, it seems simple: Life (or God) is creating through me, as me. What arises out of non-love, or perhaps a love distorted, feels stickier, harder to grasp. It confronts me with a central question: what role does seeming non-love play in my consciousness, my life, and in the world? How am I to respond to it?

I am always creating, either deliberately or unconsciously. My life is my creation; whatever I find lacking in it, I have created by default. I wish to create consciously because I'm usually not that fond of my unconscious creations.

To decide what I wish and don't wish to create, I need to feel an option to choose my inner state. Although the mechanical mind sees only one possibility, I have no real choice unless I am aware of an alternative. Any time I'm feeling less than good, I can remind myself that there is always another lens through which to see this. Although I may not be able to locate it immediately, in connecting with my willingness to find it I have already stepped out of the prison of my conditioning.

Love has a certain ease to it. Whenever I lose my ease, I am not in a state of love. Faced with a decision in such a state, I attempt to figure out the best response, forgetting that whatever I do from a place of non-love will feel good neither to me nor to another. Better to use my energy to find my way back to love, where anything I choose or create will be appropriate and helpful.

I imagine a superb furniture store with the most precious articles. I have infinite money to splurge on the very best. Loading a truck with my booty, I bring it home and cram it all into my dwelling. Although each item is a work of art, with too little space my home feels uncomfortably cramped. To sit in a living room stuffed with overabundant beauty is somehow far from relaxing. Sometimes my life exhibits the same tension. Without space, it is notably more difficult to be conscious.

The Japanese culture offers us a special gift in its exquisite use of space in gardens, paintings, and rooms. One effortlessly enters into a quiet and meditative state in the presence of such space. In the work of art that is my life, I can become more aware of the way I use inner and outer space, and how it affects my awareness.

Spaciousness contributes to clarity. My being craves space where I am neither working, doing projects, being with friends, reading, nor taking care of practical affairs. Space in the outer life allows for a spacious mind, more in touch at many levels. The conscious creation of spaciousness requires a persistent willingness to discard that which no longer serves my highest priorities.

~~~

My consciousness is like a string on a violin, designed to give forth a particular tone through vibrating at an ideal level of tension. If the string is too tight or too loose, its sound isn't right. When my string is too tight, I notice stress, agitation, addiction to movement and activity, the need for a drink, a scarcity of time to nourish the soul. What seems to help is the creation of space, less doing, and more time just being. A tight string can use some feminine spiritual energy.

When my string is too loose, I become unhealthily complacent, dull, and habitual in thought and behavior. A loose string is avoidance of the passion that can be found at the very edge of the known. Edges can be found on the emotional, intellectual, and spiritual levels. Staying too long away from edges brings a feeling of staleness in the soul, as if a window needs to be open and fresh air let in. What seems to help a loose string is finding edges to play and doing it with passion. A loose string does well with a dose of masculine spiritual energy.

MEDITATION

Although gardeners can't make things grow by themselves, they can encourage healthy growth through providing good nurturing. For the ripening of my consciousness, I want to supply the best soil possible. I fertilize it, weed it, remove unwanted pests, provide the right amount of water, and make sure the chemical balance of the soil is right for what I wish to grow. Meditation is the nurturing of my mind.

Though meditation may ultimately result in the "improvement" of my mental state, I do not undertake it in that spirit. Rather, meditation has an exploratory quality. I meditate because it is profoundly interesting. My approach is like that of a scientist, deeply involved in uncovering the secrets of the universe. Just as the scientist arises eagerly, anxious to get to the lab, I hasten daily to my "lab" of meditation, where fascinating discoveries await me.

Koans need not come from Zen masters. The best ones come out of one's own deepest inquiries. Some of mine have been: What is "now"? What is time? What is "me"? What takes place when a thought begins? What makes me want to escape this moment? What prevents peace now? What thought keeps me from loving presence?

A mind living within the prison of a limiting structure can't meaningfully conceive of freedom. It can, however, recognize and release the restrictions that bind.

Meditation isn't about the mind's content. The latter is impermanent; it comes and goes, forms and dissolves. Meditation is about the space in which all that takes place. If someone asked if I was alive now, I would instantly know the answer, even if I knew nothing else. Meditation involves locating the hum of aliveness prior to its assuming form.

What occurs when there is a concept of what meditation is supposed to feel like? A subtle effort is made to fulfill that concept: to stop thoughts, to have positive thoughts, to concentrate, to experience silence, or to reach some exalted state. Who is making these efforts? It is the "me," the being who created all the problems meditation is supposed to address. Meditation can be just another way of trying to strengthen the "me" at a more subtle level.

Meditation needs no subtle attempt to control the content of consciousness. The flow of my breath, although I am able to control it, happens quite nicely on its own without my interference. The same is true of mind; meditation can be the abandonment of the "me." When no effort is present, is there a "me"?

. . .

Since meditation is not in the realm of the known, I can't "know" how to meditate. Silence as a strategy isn't silence. Silence comes as a byproduct of understanding the limitation of thought, when all its attempts to break free are checkmated.

I can be intrigued by all sorts of techniques to refine and alter consciousness: fasting, highly developed exercise, intense breathing, long meditations, sensory deprivation, supremely focused concentration. These well-honed techniques can bring about unusual energy states of a finer vibration. My confusion arises when I view the state achieved as the means to an end: union with God, or a state of enlightenment. It is true that refining consciousness allows greater receptivity to what lies outside the limited mind. But explosion into another dimension can never be the end product of a technique.

Two of the most misconstrued words, "God" and "I," create confusion because the one isn't seen to include the other.

We are obliged by our language to talk about meditation as if it is someone looking at something. And yet where is this someone? Since the one who does the looking seems to be the repository of all fear, it might be useful to find out if this observer in fact exists.

The mind has always believed there is a "me," a thinker having thoughts, an experiencer who has experiences, a meditator meditating. A self, an ego, a something to which the word "me" refers, is assumed to exist without the slightest doubt of its reality. Without examination, this "me" feels as real as the pain of a stubbed toe. But nightmares are also experienced from within the dream as real. Could this "me" have the same reality as a nightmare?

Somewhere on my journey to awakening, it is valuable to reexamine my notion of who I am. Through meditation I come to suspect that my old conception of "me" is based on a faulty interpretation. To awaken from the nightmare requires that I be willing to release that interpretation. The challenge is that my interpretive filters operate well beneath the surface of my awareness. To release something, I must first become conscious of it.

All that the mind can conceive is that which it already knows, extrapolated a bit here and there. The thinking mind relates whatever appears in consciousness to the known; this keeps it in a conceptual prison of its own making. Freedom is possible through addressing the central question of identity—that is, by letting go of the lens through which the experience of "self" and "other" is regarded.

I make a fist, then open my hand. What happened to the fist? Did I have it and then lose it? Where is it now? These questions have no meaning, because there was really no such thing as my fist. It was a construct, a convenience of language, allowing me to freeze and describe a momentary pattern in ceaselessly flowing energy. The "me" is a similar construct.

⌒

I am tempted to think that Ego is undesirable, that the more I leave Ego behind, the more "spiritual" I am. The fact that this perspective breeds so much harshness toward myself and others gives me a loud warning that illusion is hovering nearby.

• • •

What looks upon Ego as "bad" is nothing other than Ego itself. If Ego were so regrettable, I would be obliged to oppose it; in so doing, I would hardly be demonstrating the loving acceptance entailed in an ego-free state. Harsh means cannot result in a loving end. But if Ego is an illusion, it needs no opposition; I needn't do battle against what isn't real.

Given the seeming palpability of the ego's experience, how can I know its unreality? I begin by doubting, recalling how genuine my dreams can appear. Accepting at the physical level that things are not what they seem, I remind myself that the same may be true inwardly. Once I mistrust that the "me" is what I thought it was, careful observation begins to make its unreality increasingly apparent. I see that what is called "me" is just a dream or misperception. It is not to be regretted or considered anti-spiritual, but regarded as a mere shadow, to be shone away by the light of awareness.

As my understanding blossoms, I remain comfortable in Ego's apparent presence without granting it reality. This is surely a more useful response than judging it, either in myself or in others, as bad. I take my stand that the light of love shines everywhere, that it is present without exception. I simply wish to be aware of its presence. In climbing the mountain of self-knowledge, sensing the ego's unreality is perhaps where I emerge above the timberline.

⌒

When, in the midst of this flow of energy, the question arises, "Where is the 'me' now?" the location of this entity seems remarkably elusive.

• • •

I sit down in a quiet place with the intention of freshly observing what is actually taking place in this moment. There is an awareness of an in-and-out movement that I call "breath." There is a feeling identified as "body." Now comes a sound I call "breeze," an energy burst ("I'd better get busy cleaning up my office") called "thought," which may be accompanied by emotions, fears, desires. In the Now are also reactions of liking and disliking what is happening in this flow; these are also part of the flow.

Is there actually a "someone" to whom all this is happening? Or is that "someone" just another thought? Searching in the Now for this "me," it isn't to be found. Instead, there is merely a flow of sensations, thoughts, and energy. This "me" refers to history, a set of images in time, the me of a thousand memories. "I am," the way I normally use it, is a contradiction. The "I" only exists in the past. Either "I was"; or "This!"

In the stream the water flows. Approaching a boulder, it flows around it, some to the right and some to the left. Various physical laws, such as gravity, describe this process. Gravity is not some mysterious agent causing the water to flow; it merely describes the way it flows. Is the mind, the space in which thoughts take place, any different? Is there a "me" causing the flow of thoughts? The only way to find out is to look for it. Let me see if I can find this "me" who is assumed to be creating, directing, or thinking the thoughts. It's a bit like looking for whatever is making the water flow. Searching for the "me" bears no fruit; all that appears is one thought after another. Perhaps the very seeing of this is the fruit of my search.

• • •

Could it be that I don't experience myself as loving because when love happens, it doesn't feel like "me"; and when "me" happens, it doesn't feel like love?

Can the "me" exist in the present? I think not; there can be presence, or there can be "me." Within the mystery of presence, the "me" is nowhere to be found, being built up entirely from images of the past. In short, presence and the "me" are mutually exclusive. Life is lived most consciously and fully as an anonymous being; an identity is not required, and only gets in the way.

The center of consciousness is either the time-based "me" or the Eternal Now. The first is unreal; the second is all there is. If I really understood this, I would know my true identity.

What impedes the natural flow of consciousness? Normally the attention is grabbed by the content of experience. The ego mind reacts to the content, believing that safety depends on its capacity to control the flow of events. The outcome is resistance. Without this resistance or control, is there an observer of the flow? In fact the controller, observer, and "me" are one and the same. The "me" comes into being only when there is resistance to the content of consciousness. Ego does not exist as a separate entity; it is simply the part of consciousness that tries to resist, control, or judge the flow. Although it believes itself separate from the flow it is trying to control, its attempts to control are simply part of the flow.

The world of manifestation is the surface of an ocean, always changing. That surface assumes the shape of a cloud, a mountain, a planet, a bug, a tiger, a taste, an itch . . . or a feeling of "me." That which is changing has only the limited, provisional reality of a dream. The real is eternal and indestructible.

I instinctively feel that some of what happens in consciousness is "me" and some is "not-me." I sense my leg, or a certain thought, to be inside, part of me. On the other hand, a chair's leg, or the wind outside my window, is not part of me; it is "other." In general, the body is "me" and what lies outside it is not. Is thought being arbitrary in taking for granted that I am a body? The distinction between "me" and "not-me" is an assumption worth scrutinizing.

Upon investigation, I discover that "outside" and "inside" are just concepts. There is the perception of a sound and the perception of a thought, all part of one consciousness. Without the usual labeling, what I call "the body" is just another set of sensations, another experience in consciousness. "Inside" and "outside" are ultimately ways of organizing my experience conceptually. Their actual reality is open to question.

While driving on a winding country road, I enter a meditative state in which I perceive a mystery. I see before me a road, a steering wheel, a pair of hands. The hands move the wheel, steering the car perfectly around the curves without interference from "me." The steering is subtle and precise, yet it happens by itself, just as events supposedly outside me are simply unrolling. Can I allow this mode of functioning more universally? Things seem to go better when "I" stay out of the way.

. . .

There are two aspects to my experience: one is the actual flow of moment-to-moment sensation, which any person in this situation could enjoy simply as an anonymous being, unconnected to a past. The other arises from the continuity of the self, my sense of my own "me-ness." It is governed always by my judgment of how I am doing. In which part resides the true enjoyment of life? In which part resides the stress and agony?

The ego believes in the importance of the one enjoying the experience, the "me." This becomes apparent whenever I contemplate my own death. The mind is somehow not comforted by the notion that Life will go on enjoying experiences; it thinks it intolerable that this particular "me" will no longer be present.

What is this "me" that ends when I die? Is it not simply my history? The sense of identity, of the self's continuity, arises entirely from past images. My fear of dying is proportional to the strength of my belief that I am these images.

The same factor that causes me to fear death detracts from the beauty of each moment. Whenever this "me" intrudes itself, experience loses its purity and vigor. Moments of freedom and joy happen in the Now, while the "me" dilutes this experience with the past, destroying its freshness. When experience is not related to the past, it no longer matters who is having it. The real enjoyment of life arises when the "me," with its inevitable contraction, disappears in the light of the Now.

I have faith in proportion to my sense that I am eternally safe. All the tributaries of Fear flow ultimately into the river of death, Fear's most powerful symbol. My whole sense of safety resolves ultimately to the reality or non-reality of death. If death is real for me, if "I" truly come to an end, I can't possibly feel safe, and my "faith" is just a word or symbol.

I eat too much, then experience a powerful and heavy dullness. I feel like a very old man with no desire for any aspect of life. I am aware of fear: not so much that my current state won't pass, but that it will be where I end up in this life. The thought is grim, bleak, depressing. I realize that what I am experiencing wouldn't be fearful unless I believed that at the end of that bleak period I die, and that's it. Without the fear of death, having a period like that would be a temporary interlude in eternity and wouldn't really matter. As with all my fear, I am actually experiencing the fear of death in disguise.

It feels strange to contemplate that every second, about two people die. Many billions of people have died since I was born. If animals are included, the number becomes astronomical. Common sense tells me that anything so natural and universal has got to be somehow okay. Yet most of us, unless we are very old, numbed out, greatly suffering, or somehow enlightened, view the prospect of our own death as highly undesirable. A certain farmer died in twelfth-century China. Was his death "undesirable"? Or is it just my own death that I find lamentable, or those of my loved ones? Why doesn't the death of the person called "me" feel acceptable? It makes no sense to say that some deaths are okay and some aren't. Yet the mind persists in believing otherwise, until the fundamental illusion of identity is pierced.

· · ·

Ordinarily it seems to me that my fear of death creates a clinging to life. But what if it's the other way around? What if clinging to life creates fear of death? Introspection suggests that my
death would be acceptable if the "me" weren't holding tightly
to itself. Without clinging, the ending of any particular form is
part of a natural flow, and can be accepted without fear.

To go beyond clinging requires a transformation of who I
know myself to be. Belief in the reality of death arises from a
wrong interpretation of identity. If I believe myself separate
from the Whole, then the prospect of not-being is a perpetual
danger to me. My fear of death is inevitable as long as I believe
that I am the body, a wave on the ocean of Life that must break
on shore and cease to be.

If I know myself to be part of the Whole, not-being is an alien
concept. Ending the fear of death comes only through seeing
that I am the eternal ocean of Life—the goal of all spiritual
search. Death has no meaning for the ocean, which remains at
peace while its waves break on shore.

Were I truly aware of the finitude of this particular form, I
would consider this moment precious and would inhabit it
with an appreciation normally lacking. If, after thinking I was
terminally ill, I were suddenly granted a reprieve, would I not
be filled with immense gratitude? If I passionately want to
continue living, then at some level I must be grateful for my
life. Why wait for a death sentence? Why not be fully conscious of gratitude on a daily basis?

I sit on a rocky coast and watch the sea roll in. There seem to be entities called "waves" moving from my left toward the beach on my right. Are there actual "things" moving horizontally? Looking closely I observe that any given drop of water actually moves up and down; despite appearances to the contrary, it has no horizontal movement. Amidst all this vertical movement the mind creates the illusion of an entity moving horizontally.

In similar fashion the mind creates a "thing" it calls "me." On examination, no such thing can be found; it's really just a series of events happening. To actually experience this can be an unexpected shock. It is especially striking to realize that this non-existent "me" is responsible for all my suffering, and that of the world besides. The ultimate task, if suffering is to be alleviated, is to release the belief in this "me."

Like life, the ocean changes constantly, yet remains the same. Each instant, its surface assumes a new shape. Imagine evaluating those shapes: watching the waves roll in and saying, this one is good, but I don't like the contour of that one. Accepting what is—the current shape of the ocean's surface—brings peace to my heart. The ocean is not reaching into the future toward some great climax; as in music, each moment has its own beauty in the present. Movement is happening, something which fascinates, and yet a kind of changeless pedal point persists underneath it all. As in meditation, change and changelessness are living together, lending a timeless serenity to the whole.

TIME

A seeker begins with the belief that what he wants lies in the future. If he retains that belief, he remains a seeker. If he eventually suspects that what he wants lies in the Now, he may become a finder.

The word "goal" normally implies something that I wish to occur in the future. If my goal is to be free of judgment, my ego immediately pictures itself being this way in some imaginary future. In this way, it cagily avoids serious change. Ego can now indulge its old patterns unchallenged, while continuing to assure me of the difficulty and praiseworthiness of being judgment-free. But if my goal is stripped of time, then I am willing in this moment to release judgment. Always being judgment-free seems highly daunting; but having no judgment now seems somehow doable. My "goal" of being free from judgment, purified of time, is now purified of fear.

Becoming expert at uncovering the countless ways Ego expresses itself—its endless pathology, its vast and tangled roots in the past—has not fundamentally served to end suffering. What interests me instead is a simple question: can mind be ego-free now?

.   .   .

The mind experiences life in terms of time and space. Truth, lying beyond time and space, must seemingly be stepped down to a level that the limited mind can comprehend. Caught up in illusion, the mind must speak in the vocabulary of that illusion. Yet even within the illusion, the mind has the power to move toward Truth. For example, in order to be made comprehensible, the notion of salvation—a vision of being free from my prison—is placed in the future. From within the dream I wend my way toward my future salvation.

Here is a profound and subtle challenge: when I imagine the desired breakthrough as a future attainment, I tend to live in time horizontally, wishing for it to unroll more quickly so that I may come sooner to my future release—which in the meantime I fear not attaining. A fearful means is scarcely the best path toward a loving and peaceful end.

Perhaps I would do better to orient myself vertically. I suspect that what I so eagerly await lies here with me in this moment, underneath my fear. I relax and open to it, trusting in the rhythm of its unfolding. I can find comfort in the moment by diving underneath discomfort the way I dive down into the ocean under a big wave. I can console myself in my suffering by thinking of my freedom; but it is truer, and feels better, to conceive of this freedom as present in the Eternal Now, into which I can always safely relax.

If peace is attainable, it's attainable for me. If it's attainable for me, it's available to me Now. Were I really to believe that, I might release some of my resistance to letting it in.

Impatience is longing, with the unnecessary addition of time.

We often think of "waiting" as an unpleasant activity: waiting in line, waiting for someone who's late. Yet we spend a good deal of our life waiting: for the evening, the weekend, the vacation, the promotion, the perfect relationship. By calling all this "waiting," I imply that the significance of this moment lies entirely in the future toward which it is leading. In doing so, I essentially dismiss much of life as insignificant.

Spirituality is not something I work at, in order to get better at it. My ego loves the concept of "progress"; I hold it up as an ideal, measure myself against it, and usually find myself (and therefore others) severely wanting. I fail to understand that the opportunity to be spiritual is Now. Any time I become aware that I haven't been living my vision, I can always rectify that by bringing an attitude of loving acceptance to this moment.

All consciousness takes place within the Now. Yet when the mind tries to conceive of the present moment, all it can think of is an infinitesimal slice between the past and future. The Now can be experienced in its infinite variety, but it cannot be conceived. Conception is time. What is there about Now that I can never leave it? What is there about Now that I can never grasp and hold it? The ego's conception of Now is a snapshot that freezes the flow of events, then tries to define them. When attention is seized by thought, the Now is infinitely small; when attention is on the flow of what is, the Now is infinitely large. In the shift from the former to the latter lies a profound secret of meditation.

One can experience the mysterious phenomenon of the Eternal Now, constantly changing yet always the same. The present is generally conceived of as somehow being like a still picture, frozen in time. Yet an attempt to capture the present moment finds everything in flux. Change is normally thought to require time. How can the present include change?

I imagine riding a surfboard on the top of a moving wave. With reference to the shore, I am moving; with reference to the wave, I remain in the same place. Like the wave, the Now is always moving. Thoughts come and go, with silence behind and between. Living in the Eternal Now means that awareness rides the crest of the moving wave.

One second ago is more like ten years ago than it is like now.

The experience of life is never the past or the future; it is always in the Eternal Now. So how do I conceive of the notion of Now when there is never an occasion when it isn't Now? Where is the Not-Now with which to contrast it? One may ask, what about the past and future? The mind catches itself slipping endlessly into the memory of the past, or the imagination of the future, complaining, "It's so hard to be in the Now; it seems to require such vigilance and focus." But memory and imagination are merely the content of thought, and that thought is still happening now. I am not generally aware of its "now-ness," because I am hypnotized by the content. The movement from being under the spell of thought to awareness of Now occurs instantaneously and without effort, in the moment that there is awareness of having been caught up in mental activity.

I can never—no matter how much I manipulate the content of my thoughts—leave the Eternal Now. It may take remembering to be aware that it is Now, but no effort is required to be there, since it's already the case.

Another interesting question: who is it that can't leave the Eternal Now? This is a good jumping-off point for meditation.

⟋

Going for a walk in the lovely countryside, I suddenly become aware that I've missed the surrounding beauty for the last mile. Immediately, I become upset with myself . . . yet why do I waste energy fighting against what is already gone? Beauty abounds in *this* moment. Am I letting it in?

My reality is re-created each instant; it can change dramatically in the blink of an eye. Yet actual transformation of consciousness is rare, because the vast majority of my re-creations are virtually the same as the moment before.

In the midst of change, does my experience include that which is beyond change? My attention is normally captured by the changing world of form. But the mind wonders: is there a changeless something out of which breath, thought, and experience arise? A wave is a disturbance in water. A thought is a disturbance in . . . something. What is that something?

·   ·   ·

When I don't like the current content of my consciousness because the sense impressions are ugly, the body is in pain, or fear is casting a shadow, there is value in shifting my attention away from the moving content in the foreground of my awareness to the formless, unchanging current in the background. I shift my attention to the space in which all of this moving content is happening, pure being in its most universal aspect. Within this space is an underlying current of energy before it takes on the form of thoughts, feelings, or sensations. The simple energy of pure being is the current of Life, anonymous and loving, the source of my individual life. The mystery of existence dwells in this current.

As I open to this deeper level, I feel my fundamental contraction relaxing and softening. It feels like a preparation for the ultimate relaxation into pure Being. If some part of my awareness remains with the pure hum of Being, I am less likely to get swept away by the drama of thoughts and events. Equanimity arises when my interest shifts from what is unique in each moment to what is common to every moment.

After a long walk, I sit on the banks of a peaceful stream. Softening, entering the timeless flow, I observe myself gazing into the moving water in two distinct ways. First, my eyes follow a particular bubble as it is swept along. They follow it until the bubble disappears or leaves my field of vision, at which point my gaze sweeps swiftly back to fix on another bubble, again following it briefly on its journey. But sometimes I perceive the moving stream in a different way: I keep my eyes fixed on a single spot in front of me while the bubbles flow by. The attention refuses to be caught up in the bubbles. Shifting from the first way of looking to the second transforms the way time is perceived. Instead of being hypnotized by the bubble of thought as it moves through time, my attention remains focused on a fixed spot and thus remains effortlessly in the present. As the stream ripples by, my inner landscape flows on from Now to Now.

III

SELF-MASTERY

DESIRE

My desire is not to be perfect, but rather to deal gracefully with imperfection.

My body needs nourishment, so I satisfy my hunger. In that lies no conflict. The problem begins with craving beyond physical satisfaction. I associate food with pleasure, relaxation, and security, and use it in an effort to achieve these states. Of course, it never brings me the comfort I yearn for. All I succeed in doing is dulling out the sharpest pangs of desire. The deeper pain remains beneath.

The difficulty is compounded when I react against the habit of overeating. Knowing that overeating is good neither for the body nor for the mind's clarity, I impose on myself the commandment Thou shalt not overeat. Between the craving and the commandment lies my battlefield. Somewhere along the way, a healthy impulse—the wish to eat sanely—gets translated into a "should." It feels like I have a harsh inner parent ordering me around. Instead of loving encouragement from within, I feel it as an imposed limitation on what I crave. Inevitably, the child within rebels.

. . .

I have a desire to indulge in unhealthy activity, followed by a wave of guilt and a belief that I shouldn't have such a desire. Repressing my craving will often lead to its ultimate unhealthy indulgence. Repressing and indulging are opposite sides of the same coin; both grant the desire undue importance. Repressing my desire is closer to indulging it than to ignoring it.

How can I continue to indulge in harmful behavior that I know I will regret later? My ego has its own version of "living in the Now," which expresses itself the way a child demands immediate gratification, oblivious to the consequences. Today I can eat or drink to excess, ignoring the fact that the one who will suffer indigestion or a hangover tomorrow is still me. This is the same mind-set that ignores long-range social or environmental consequences in favor of the quick fix.

This not-caring about another is actually much the same whether the "other" is me in the future or another human being, one who also calls himself "I" and has to live with the consequences of my self-centeredness. In both cases, the "other" is felt as an abstraction rather than as a real person who suffers. Who really cares about abstractions? The "me" of tomorrow, suffering with hypertension or clogged arteries, this "me" whom I so glibly ignore in my choices today, isn't fundamentally different from the "me" in another body experiencing the painful consequences of my ecological, economic, or personal greed.

⁓

I wish to respond intelligently to my desires. This necessitates being fully aware of them, sensing which ones are healthy, and nourishing those. It also means believing that I deserve to have them fulfilled, as well as freedom from the sabotage of an unconscious desire for the contrary. Finally, sensing the truth that like attracts like, I need to be energetically in alignment with what I want, desiring with strength, clarity, and purity. To attract positive results requires a positive state of mind. When my mind is not clear, when it is clouded by fear or a sense of lack, then the flame of desire is laced with the smoke of confusion. Desire is purified when it emanates from a state of present satisfaction. The key to attracting what I truly want is to be comfortable now, desiring with enthusiasm instead of fear.

I am made duller by the incessant feeding of desires. I may make myself so dull that I feel the urge for intense or unusual experiences in order to feel the passion of living. I may seek a new and stimulating environment in exotic places. Yet, after a while, the newness wears off and I encounter the same old attitude: tomorrow I'm going to visit some other place even more beautiful, or experience something even more thrilling.

I imagine that I have been a prisoner for many years, believing myself doomed to spend the rest of my days in an airless cell. Then, suddenly, I am given my freedom. The very first day, I take a walk, hear the birds and the sound of wind anew, take pleasure from observing people, the lighting of the sky, the trees, and the delicious fragrance of fresh air. My cells are vibrating with the fullness of life.

My daily life, though free, is missing this sheer existential joy; I fail to take in the beauty that surrounds me. Were I open to receive it, such would be my daily diet. The mind mistakenly translates my yearning for this aliveness into a desire for a particular experience: a delicious meal, an exotic vacation. In this way I diminish and trivialize the depth of my yearning.

It is vital to yearn for the experience of my connection to the Whole. Seeing the overriding importance of that, I realize that none of my specific desires is essential to my overall well-being and happiness. Free of attachment, I can enjoy the fulfillment of such desires without giving any of them undue importance.

⁓

What role does desire play in my journey to the deepest Truth? Is it a hindrance on the path? Are all desires, including spiritual ones, merely manifestations of the "me" impotently trying to escape its uncomfortable prison? Or is there a class of desire that serves me well on my journey, such as a desire for Truth or enlightenment, a desire to be free of suffering?

I experience three kinds of desire. The first arises from the body and its legitimate needs. No conflict there. The second is more troublesome, emanating from my fundamental discomfort in just being. Cravings for sensory and emotional gratification, or security, serve as an ever-hopeful escape from my distress. Their fruits never satisfy for long. Because such desires include a resistance to the current moment, along with attachment to a future form, they serve to increase my overall level of anxiety.

The third kind of desire, however, is a yearning from the deepest recess of my soul. I desire to feel love in my heart, to use my natural talents in the service of the whole. This kind of desire is indeed compatible with total acceptance of this moment. Therefore it can organize and focus my energy without strengthening the ego.

When aligned with my Deeper Wisdom, I am driven by my passion rather than enticed by what I think I lack. My enthusiasm is not for the final attainment of my desire, but for the sheer process of making it manifest. I will act out of my deepest instinct and then let go, confident that something interesting will happen. Since my survival and safety aren't dependent on the precise result, the whole proceeding is more like play. I can be like the child who joyfully builds a sand castle directly in front of the incoming tide.

My essence yearns, my ego craves: the two have a different flavor. Healthy yearning is the energy of Life attracted to love, joy, and creation. I can be aware—in this moment—of a yearning to feel connected to my Source. It is not a conceptual longing for a future state, but an opening now to the possibility of knowing that connection. My longing is a prayer arising from my very depths. Love is calling gently back to me from what I was meant to become. When I allow it, my energy flows and I am filled with enthusiasm and passion. It is good to be on intimate and loving terms with my yearnings. They enlighten me about my true purpose and bring direction to my life.

Sensing my own numbness, I become aware that I'd like to be able to feel more fully. But when I say that, I mean one of two things: either "I'd kind of like to, but it's not that important to me"; or "No, this is really important to me, I really want to be able to feel fully!" If I say it the second way, with feeling, am I not right then, in the strength of my desire, feeling fully?

⌒

Discontent and desire are opposite sides of a single coin. Both engender suffering until they are purified. They are purified when stripped of the resistance that normally accompanies them. With desire, the resistance may not be as obvious. Yet most desire, when examined deeply, is accompanied by a feeling that something is missing; I want out of this moment, and desire is my means. Discontent and desire are both purified by fully accepting my present state. Anger and frustration become Divine Discontent; the sadness of unfulfillment is transformed into Pure Longing.

I conclude that there is no purpose to my life, and become depressed. Then I ask myself, is it okay with me that I have no purpose? The answer is no. I wish to feel passion and direction in my life, and am discontented because I do not. Yet this very discontent is my way out of the dilemma. Discontent can become passion when purified and allowed to flower without leaking away through self-pity, distraction, or drugs. It is in my power to allow my discontent to be transformed into passion. Whoever wants something with passion has a purpose.

Pleasure is the ego's version of feeling good. There is nothing wrong on any level with feeling good; but pleasure as experienced by Ego is shallow to begin with, and, since it is never enough, it always carries the seeds of dissatisfaction. Why settle for pleasure? Why not go for feeling deeply good?

.   .   .

Pleasure is not experienced now; it always involves anticipation or remembrance. Perhaps this statement, which may sound less than obvious, needs to be tested by investigation. What happens in the midst of pleasure? The minute I become conscious that I am having pleasure (rather than just being the experience), the mind is thinking, which means it is no longer fully present with the experience. Thinking leads to plotting how to have more intense pleasure, more frequent pleasure, more predictable pleasure, less time without pleasure. This process takes over the mind, and the original enjoyment is lost.

Is happiness the point of it all? The limitations of language may create confusion. It is useful to distinguish between deep happiness and superficial happiness. The former is a feeling of profound well-being, transcending surface moods, without external causation or opposite. It arises when I am in a state of perfect love, or when I am clear about what I am here to do and then do it. I experience deep happiness when I am aware of being on the path to which my destiny has called me.

Surface happiness alternates with its opposite: sadness, or incompleteness. As Nisargedatta Maharaj has said, between the banks of happiness and sadness the river of life flows. Wishing to be "happy" all the time is desiring day without night, inhaling without exhaling. But we are designed for a deeper kind of happiness, which includes both comfortable and uncomfortable feelings.

⌒⌐

I come home from a social gathering feeling vaguely uncomfortable. The source of my uneasiness is my unmet social agenda, which may include being properly liked, entertained, listened to, agreed with, or respected. The strength of my agenda—which is really an agenda for others—is proportional to my feeling of inadequacy. To release it, I remind myself before going out that I expect nothing from anybody at this gathering. The thought may not be 100 percent effective in vanquishing my fear, but it helps me relax and enjoy myself in surprising ways.

This doesn't mean I am free of desire. Although I may want nothing from you, I most certainly want something from the Universe. The difference is that the Universe is always able to give it, whereas you are not. Life unfolds more gracefully when I allow the Universe a wide latitude in the ways it may satisfy my yearnings.

A life of Spirit shifts attention away from form. There can be no satisfaction without a full awareness of the space in which all form comes and goes. My task is to uncover the single assumption that gives rise to my suffering: the belief that I am separate from my Source. By challenging the validity of this belief and letting it go, I may come again to know the connection that has never been severed.

My deepest longings may be hidden from my awareness because of a belief that I don't deserve what I want, or that it isn't possible for me to have it. I am far more likely to attract what I truly want if I feel that I deserve it. Such a feeling arises not from an act of volition, but from having dissolved my feeling of unworthiness. Getting in touch with what I truly want can itself be a major step on the road to attaining it.

. . .

Once I establish my longing, there are several places to investigate should it fail to materialize. Perhaps my desire is in conflict with another, less conscious opposing one. For example, my desire to lose weight may be opposed by the contrary desire to eat whatever I want, whenever I want, as much as I want.

Is what I call my desire really what I want? Lukewarm or conflicted desire has little attracting power. Doubting that I deserve or can have what I desire produces the same result as not desiring it at all. Perhaps I don't desire purely and passionately enough. Desire can be intensified and purified by imagining daily the way life would be if I had what I truly wish for, cherishing it lovingly in my mind and heart. For example, if I desire to live in a beautiful place, I might imagine regularly what it feels like to look out the window at the shapely hills, to step outside the front door, surrounded by beauty, and breathe the pure air. With this constant watering, the plant will flourish.

THE LAW OF ATTRACTION

For living in the world of dualism, of preference, The Law of Attraction has proven an unmistakably useful teaching. It asserts that like attracts like at all levels of energy. Life shows us effortlessly how matter attracts matter. It takes a while longer to learn that like attracts like in the world of thought and behavior. Observation does reveal that the focus of my attention reflects what I give importance to and attracts more of the same.

To improve any situation, I determine what I want as the outcome and then demonstrate that quality now. Since what I ultimately want is love, choosing a loving response to this moment places me in harmony with what I want and tends therefore to attract it.

As within, so without. The outer is a powerful reflection of the inner. I examine the content of my outer life so as to better understand the content of my inner. A chaotic exterior will reflect a chaotic interior, while an inner harmony will tend to manifest itself outwardly.

·   ·   ·

Every action, word, or thought has the potential to strengthen some part of me. Am I nourishing the outlook I would consciously choose to promote? When I lack awareness, I tend to reinforce my old mental habits. I can tell what kind of attitude I am energizing by how my life looks and by how I feel. As I get older, my physical appearance reflects it as well. The viewpoint I continually nourish will attract the quality of my life.

⁓

In the aftermath of an uncomfortable occurrence, I tend to view my role with either guilt or denial: either I deserve this misfortune, or I am a pure victim of it. A more useful response would be to say "I seem to have attracted this; I wonder how *that* happened."

A favorite trick of Fear is to tell me that, although my goal is attainable in theory, its pursuit will require a severe and arduous effort, involving much suffering on the way to a highly dubious outcome. Such an attitude becomes a self-fulfilling prophecy.

It's tempting to believe that my emotions accurately reflect what is going on around me, that I am upset because upsetting things are happening. I may use a partner's behavior as an excuse to keep myself from feeling good: "I can't be happy now because of your mood." In truth, what my feelings inform me about most accurately is the attitude with which I greet the world.

Underneath all my superficial desires lies the yearning to feel connected to my Source. Sadness, anger, or discontent means I am not allowing myself to receive the universal nourishment that is always available. When I am feeling love, peace, joy, it is because I am allowing it. If I am not allowing this moment to nourish me, my discomfort tells me that I need an attitudinal shift. What I experience moment to moment is largely my response to my own beliefs.

⁓

At a gourmet banquet, I don't fill my plate with potato chips. Yet, in the banquet of life, I may entertain a good deal of mental junk food: "Oh, God, when I get home, she's not going to like this. . . ." "We're not going to have enough money to. . . ." "This is going to be really hard. . . ." "Why does this always have to happen to me?" "Junk" thoughts include all the things I dwell on that I don't want to happen. Understanding the Law of Attraction brings another level of vigilance toward the toxic thoughts that I have left unchallenged in my mind.

Speech can also be an unconscious manifestation of negative energy. Every time I catch myself about to say something negative, I make a conscious choice about the kind of energy I wish to put out into the world. My conditioned mind dwells chiefly in a kind of default setting, until I realize that I can choose consciously where to put my attention. No matter how upset I am, an inner choice is always available in the moment that will allow me to feel more at peace. To find it, I have to believe that such a choice is available and be willing to uncover it. Becoming conscious of my thoughts and words gives me power over the quality of my outer and inner life.

⁓

Is it my job to make others feel good? If I believe so, I will experience frequent failure and frustration. If I am attached to results, I defeat my own purpose. My real task is to bring a loving presence to each moment, trusting others to create a path that's right for themselves.

Do I truly know what another's path should look like? I may say to my child, "You're really screwing up. Your life is a mess, and you'd better get it together. Here's what you need to do." Or I may say "I see you having difficulties, but I trust you to make your own mistakes and learn from them. You have your own guidance system and it will serve you well. I love you and support you." Which approach will ultimately be more helpful to my child?

Does the gap between present reality and my intention imply that a fierce battle must rage within, over which one will prevail? I think not. The part of me that dwells in Truth has no need to struggle against the false. To have dominance in my consciousness, however, my Deeper Wisdom does need to be "fed" through persistent awareness of its presence. Whatever I nourish regularly in myself will grow strong.

There are but two basic feelings: one feels good, the other doesn't. The one that feels good is love; the one that doesn't can be seen as yearning for love.

⁓

I recall from childhood my mother pouring iodine on my cuts. I remember howling with pain. One day, she tells me the pain I am experiencing is actually the agony of the germs being killed. It dramatically changes my whole experience. Instead of feeling like a passive victim, I actually relish my pain with the gleeful thought: "Take that!"

Perhaps at some level, the situations I find offensive are all " iodine" awaiting an attitudinal shift. The pain of someone not liking me, for example, can be a healing force if I allow it to teach me. Instead of germs being killed, it is the false beliefs that have festered inside me.

Painful emotional states can be the kind of adversity that strengthens. I imagine being a runner who practices mostly on easy, level trails in favorable weather. But every once in a while I run up into the mountains on a cold day, chugging uphill with a strong wind blowing in my face and a forty-pound pack on my back. It's far more arduous, but in this way I acquire the gift of strength and endurance, as well as a certain satisfaction in being a warrior. Seeking a healthy attitude in the midst of difficult feelings is effective resistance training.

PERSONAL STRENGTH

Which would I prefer: for my feelings to be at the mercy of outside forces, or to be free and the master of my own experience? If I refuse to take responsibility for my feelings, then I am choosing the former; I am confining myself to the lifetime role of victim. My honest answer to the question "Who do I believe causes my suffering?" is an excellent barometer of my potential for freedom.

Powerful inner evidence suggests that my discomfort arises not from circumstances, but from how my mind responds to them. I create my own bad or good feeling by my simple choice of whether to close my heart or allow love to flow. Whenever I enter into discord with another, I may safely assume full responsibility for my discomfort. Had I greeted whatever happened lovingly, I would have been at peace. For all of my own history—and that of humankind—the momentum has been to close it, so I need a little practice in making the other choice. Being responsible is the best possible news, because it means I can release victimhood for once and for all, and take charge of my life. Every time I refuse to succumb to my belief in my own victimhood, I erode a portion of the wall that keeps me from my Loving Truth.

· · ·

A major attribute of victimhood is its powerful attraction. Once I have taken offense, I observe my strange reluctance to let it go. If I look honestly within, I will likely find a part of me that takes pleasure in blaming my partner, boss, family, neighbors, or the system for my frustrations. Although it's hard to admit, my ego takes comfort in the role of injured and misunderstood victim.

I see people around me doing this—blaming others for their suffering and enjoying it—and I become annoyed. Why is this? Could it be that I am looking into a mirror? I fail to see that whenever I get upset at someone else, I give that person the power to take away my peace. I base my own equanimity on their love, their sensitivity to my needs, or their agreement with my values. In this, am I not being a victim myself?

At times, I find passivity in others to be maddening, and I become upset. In losing my peace simply because someone else is being who they are, I fail to realize that I am indulging my own passivity. Rather than setting my own emotional tone, I am allowing it to be determined by another. Whenever I believe someone has to behave in a loving or emotionally mature manner to ensure my comfort, I am demonstrating the very thing I'm objecting to. At the core of the ego lies a belief in one's victimhood.

Resentment is weakness disguised as strength. Would I resent another if I didn't believe he or she had the power to make me feel bad? Resentment and victimhood are twin aspects of one state. The latter disguises and perpetuates itself through the former. The antidote to both is true strength.

· · ·

Victimhood is often characterized by a sense of "I have to." I have to remain in this unsatisfactory marriage, or job. I have to feel bad when someone is angry with me. I have to spend time doing what I don't like. The mechanical mind believes either that some outside agent is compelling me, or that I simply can't help my own reactions. My partner gets upset with me, and my closed-hearted reaction feels impossibly distant from a choice. It comes as a powerful revelation to realize that everything I do, outwardly or inwardly, is in fact a choice, although often an unconscious one. The experience of choice begins when consciousness arises.

A way out of victimhood is to understand that I am choosing to do whatever I am doing now. A moment from now, I will be free to make another choice. The choices may involve my outer or my inner life: I may choose whether or not to remain in a job or a relationship. But I may also choose to accept a situation that is impossible to change. Mastery over my inner landscape is gained by learning to make such choices consciously.

I find myself in an unhappy state and want to get rid of it. I am unable to do so, and become angry with myself for this failure. My anger has a feeling of impotent rage; it has a whiney quality to it, underneath. Although I believe I am angry because I want my negativity to be gone, my anger at my current state is, in truth, merely an extension of it. Truly wanting negativity to be gone results in a different response, one that accepts the way I am feeling in the moment while refusing to support or indulge my negative thinking.

. . .

When self-judgment ends, so does victimhood. Feeling unlovable, I seek worthiness from another, feeling hurt or angry when they are unable to provide it. I have made myself a victim. As soon as I provide love for myself, the other loses the power to make me unhappy.

⌒

To feel "betrayed" is not a perception, but an interpretation—one that does not serve. Feeling betrayed implies that my happiness and well-being are dependent on someone else's behavior.

Many are the occasions when I look forward to feeling good and am disappointed. A bit less common are the times when I expect not to feel good and am pleasantly surprised. Both cases clearly demonstrate how my inner landscape trumps outer circumstances. Here lies the path to true strength.

When I complain, in addition to creating a toxic atmosphere, I keep my discontent from serving its proper function. Discontent is meant to build until it explodes into useful action or an attitudinal shift. Complaining inhibits this process when the pressure that is meant to accumulate instead leaks out in useless grumbling. For example, an employer who complains about his employee forestalls more positive outcomes: firing the employee, learning to accept the employee the way he or she is, or having a serious conversation that leads either to improvement or termination.

Casual conversation in my home may involve my partner and me finding something mutually annoying and complaining about it. Such exchanges exacerbate the general feeling of victimhood, as well as teaching children powerlessness. (Children's whining imitates their elders' complaining.) I find it instructive to have formal days of no complaining. When I find myself about to complain, I take a snapshot of my inner landscape, which helps me challenge my ego's belief in victimhood.

When I'm not doing very well, I sometimes find the innocent question "How are you?" creating a dilemma. Two common responses present themselves, neither feeling right. I may begin listing all the things that are going wrong, unleashing a barrage of unwanted negative energy and emphasizing my belief in victimhood. I don't like myself in this mode. On the other hand, the stoic response, the casual "I'm okay," while sparing the other my unpleasant outburst, feels like a lie. Is there a way to avoid both these less-than-satisfying alternatives?

When I do not feel like the victim of my difficulties, I am more apt to respond realistically, without going to either extreme. A friend asks me how my week went. "Well, I had a really big challenge. A close friend was quite hard on me in a way that seemed unfair. I've been feeling angry. I'm trying to understand what I'm meant to learn from all this, but haven't got a handle on it yet." This forthright description of my feelings, balancing and humanizing, is easier for friends to hear than either my stoicism or my complaining.

⟜⟋

My deepest intentions arise from the depth of Life. Whenever I align my intention with that of the Universe, nothing but good can arise.

.   .   .

Intention is the balancing force of surrender. A wise balance of surrender and intention helps me in bringing positive change to my life.

To be effective, my desire to feel more harmony and joy in my life needs to be accompanied by persistent, focused intention. This is the quality of a warrior—someone who takes a stand and persists in the face of obstacles, mistakes, and forgetting. To be effective, intention must be as vigorous as its opposing forces. It must also be undiluted by the unconscious contradictory pull that can undermine it. Unless intention is well developed, I am overwhelmed by the powerful winds of daily life against which I'm sailing; I tend to get blown off course by old habits. With fully awakened intention, I find that self-pity and helplessness give way to a growing sense of self-mastery.

A man gets angry and hits his wife. Later he offers the excuse that he didn't really mean to. Yet by his actions he has revealed the insufficiency of his intention: he has never taken his stand that it is simply not okay for him to resort to physical violence. The same applies to the violence of words or gestures. If I wish to free myself of all that, then I must take my stand. I take it whenever I am tempted to blame another for my suffering, yet refuse to adopt that position. I take it whenever inner or outer discipline is difficult and I do it anyway. I take my stand that love is present now, and that I deserve it. Without taking my stand, my life is just a mechanical re-creation of the role my family and culture have already assigned me. Taking one's stand is essential to a life of freedom.

.   .   .

Expectation is the Ego's version of intention. Expectation declares "I'm holding that this had better happen in this particular way; if it doesn't, I'm going to be really upset." Intention says "I have a vision I intend to create. I'll give it my best and then let go of any attachment to a specific form."

For every moment of frustration or helplessness, an intention lies waiting. After dwelling for a time in an uncomfortable state, I reach a place where I become really sick of it. At this point I am tempted to feel like a victim, or to disparage myself for not being able to break out of my suffering. I am not making proper use of my profound discontent. "I'm really sick of this!" fulfills its function when it transforms itself into "I intend to find a way to release this!"

If I care to accomplish something, I need to be aware of my level of intention. When I say "I wish I could do that" in a sighing and hopeless voice, or "I'll try to do it," I support the belief that my capacity to succeed is easily overwhelmed by circumstances beyond my control. I feel noticeably stronger in mind and body when I assert "That's something I intend to do."

The natural outcome of healthy discontent is intention. The outcome of unhealthy self-criticism is paralysis. I tell myself "I'm so self-centered (or judgmental, or unaware, or incompetent)"; or I hear myself repeating the common phrase "I can't express my feelings." In limiting myself to such definitions, I am reciting a mantra that defines the situation, binds me by its constraint, and helps perpetuate what isn't wanted. Unconscious negativity lurks in the vocabulary of thought and leads to a self-fulfilling outcome. A more useful alternative is the statement: "I intend to learn how to express my feelings despite any obstacles."

～

Normally, what passes for spontaneity—action resulting from surrender to the moment—is actually reaction, a passive expression of my conditioning. If I am deeply ensconced in habits of thinking, feeling, and acting that arise from the momentum of fear, I require something to thrust me beyond my conditioning. That something is intention. Without it, my seemingly "spiritual" gesture of letting go will be a mere surrender to habit. True spontaneity requires not only surrender to the moment, but also saying No to weary old patterns, so the fresh energy of Life may flow creatively through me.

I go on a meditation retreat and find it deeply fulfilling. I conclude that I want to include more meditation in my daily existence. Returning to my ordinary life, I find that I am taken over by its vicissitudes. There are too many phone calls, letters, obligations; I don't seem to have sufficient time for meditation. At this point, I create the intention to meditate every morning. I make an agreement with myself to do this in the face of my own resistance and the excuse that there isn't time. Were I to meditate "spontaneously"—i.e., only when I was in the mood—my practice would be very irregular, and it would not serve me nearly so well. Through a certain discipline, I achieve a greater measure of freedom.

Exercise teaches me much about the limitations of my so-called spontaneity. Despite my intention and the pleasure I know I will take from it, I often have to overcome a strong reluctance to begin a workout. The body is tired and the mind endlessly creative in its array of excuses of why this really isn't a good time. Yet I often manage to coax myself into action by assuring myself that I'll stop if I'm still tired after five minutes. This occurs with surprising infrequency, however, as I reap the benefit of consistency. Once again discipline, triumphing over spontaneity, brings freedom.

The path to full consciousness can be seen as a movement from false to true spontaneity, with a period of conscious inhibition in the middle. Let's say I start off addicted to sweets, salt, or fat. Left to my own devices, I reach "spontaneously" for these unhealthful foods. Later, I try out more healthful options and find that I feel better. I nevertheless find that old impulses die hard, and for a time I battle with myself to eat healthfully. Only my strong intention keeps me going; it is my temporary substitute for true spontaneity. Finally, my body and whole being move up the spiral, and I begin to crave only healthful food. Once again, I am eating spontaneously, but now in alignment with my body's wisdom.

When I am in conflict about what to do, it is important to eschew the seeming spontaneity of doing whatever my ego believes will bring gratification in the moment. True freedom is found when my choice is voluntarily given over to a higher and wiser part of my being. My Deeper Wisdom always intuits correct action.

I tell myself that I want to clean the basement. Yet, weeks and months go by and the basement remains a mess because of one simple fact: I am not whole-hearted about wanting to clean it. Although part of me wants to, a larger part of me, perhaps not fully acknowledged, doesn't. What a difference when I am feeling whole! When I am excited about a project, I wake up every morning thinking about it enthusiastically. I find the energy to organize my time around it with no trouble. It's clear that when I'm one hundred percent into something, I do it.

In order to avoid immediate conflict, I make agreements without the intention to keep them. The result is broken agreements. Whenever I don't keep an agreement I can usually look back and observe that I made it without fully intending to honor it.

⟜

Passion for life depends on a sense of meaning. Meaning derived from outward beauty, intelligence, success, and so on is always in danger of being taken away; if by nothing else, then certainly through age. As they age, many people experience a sense of life collapsing without youth to uphold it. I wish to have a sense of meaning that can't be taken from me.

Where would such a sense of meaning come from? It might be described as connecting with the Source, learning to love more perfectly, or using one's natural talents to promote the good of the Whole. If I have such a sense of meaning and can connect it to what's happening from moment to moment, I will be more fully present for my life. I tend to be naturally present when something matters.

Something matters to me either because I am interested in what is actually happening in the moment, or because of the outcome I hope it will bring. Such an outcome may involve simple personal gain, but it may also involve my conception of some ultimate greater good. But although future-based meaning can produce a certain feeling of aliveness, it also carries with it the fear that my desired outcome won't materialize. This fear, which is pervasive in my consciousness, prevents me from enjoying my moment-to-moment existence. The activist, scientist, therapist, or artist may do work that serves a greater good. Yet if they become attached to the fruits of their labor, and therefore work in a state of constant anxiety, they may ultimately lose the creative spark in their work.

Ultimately, my strongest sense of meaning comes from my interest in the moment, in and of itself. When I care about something for its own sake, my passion is free of the fear that so often accompanies it. The key is giving each moment my loving presence. Placing my interest here, rather than in any outcome, breeds freshness and creativity. Each meditation, each hearing of the same piece of music, each walk down the familiar road, each hug or sexual connection, can be experienced as if for the first time.

A major source of meaning arises from the fact that Love is always looking for ways to expand itself. One opportunity for its enhancement lies in seeking out the places where it seems at the moment not to be, and then finding love in those places. Coming in from a heavy rain, I feel the peaceful glow of finally becoming warm and dry. In truth, I was warm and dry before I went out, but failed to notice or appreciate it. In moments of clarity I see that there is no place in the Universe devoid of love; but the confused ego mind creates the illusion of non-love. The dissipation of that illusion allows the experience of love to expand and increase.

Why is depression so pervasive in our culture? Perhaps most of us are not connected to our true destiny. When we fail to locate our passion and to place it at the center of our life, we invite depression at some level. If we have a strong spiritual sensibility, but it remains unfocused, we may be all the more susceptible. A life of the spirit can only be a primary focus; it cannot be casual.

I can picture myself as a cell in a large body called the human race. Like everyone, I have a certain function that I have been designed for. Living well involves determining what kind of a cell I am and making sure my life expresses its essential function. Whenever I do what I am designed to do, in harmony with the Whole, I feel energy, joy, and a sense of rightness.

IV

TOWARD
SELF-COMPASSION

To turn my love toward myself is not an egoic gesture, but a deep appreciation of the unique beauty of this person. Self-love is quite distinct from arrogance or selfishness.

Self-judgment is a painful detour on the path to self-knowledge. In fact, what most prevents my seeing deeply into my core is feeling bad about myself. My very desire to be free of judgment may slip inadvertently into judging myself for my failure to do so. If I know in advance that I will be harsh with myself for my failings, I won't allow myself to see them for fear of my self-flagellation. Thus I become blind to the judgments I myself make.

To release these judgments, I must first become aware of them. This will be easier if I decide in advance to be kind to myself for every manifestation of Ego, seeing that all fear-based behavior deserves an equally compassionate response. Compassion for myself needs especially to include my imperfections, allowing me to know that I won't blame myself if I make a mistake. Refusing to entertain self-judgment is of great help toward making the unconscious conscious, toward releasing what no longer serves.

· · ·

On occasion, the unconscious mind will reveal its contents like a camera opening its shutter for the briefest instant. When a friend tells me of his good fortune, my envious mind responds with a spark of resentment: I am actually disappointed. This is followed instantly by "I didn't think that! I'm really happy for him." The whole thing takes place in a flash, almost too rapidly to notice. With lightning speed, my mind snaps on the lid to bury such a gross, ungenerous, blatantly self-centered thought. This allows me to maintain my image of myself as basically a pretty nice person. Unless I am supremely alert, this rapid squelching of what I disapprove of in myself remains buried and I delude myself into thinking I am more consistently kind than I really am.

⌒

At an early age, the mind, in order to feel safe, adopts a strategy for emotional survival. A typical strategy is to act nicer than one feels. Given the circumstances of childhood, there is inevitably a kind of wisdom in such a policy. Yet the same mind later asserts that I am bad for losing my integrity! Having decided on a survival strategy, it now decides that I should feel guilty for having adopted it.

Fear tells me that closing my heart will keep me safe. After I obey its command, Fear reacts: "What's the matter with you? Why can't you be more loving?" Or the mind enticingly suggests "Oh, go ahead, have another helping," and then later scolds, "You shouldn't have done that!" I fail to see that it's the same voice speaking. First it suggests indulging fear or desire, then it blames me for so doing so.

. . .

Whenever I pass judgment on myself, I am pretending that the one judging is somehow different from the one being judged. Here lies the great error upon which guilt is founded: the mind's division into judge and judged. It's interesting to ask myself, Who is judging whom? Self-judgment requires that I divide myself in two: the rider with the crop, and the horse who is whipped; the magistrate with the privilege and right to condemn, and the convict who believes he deserves punishment. In fact both are one: the judge merely entertains the absurd belief that it is separate from the entity who performed the act. Thought first creates an identity, an "I," from past images, and then attacks it. One thought is simply opposing another. To play this bizarre game, I must consent to the rules.

To counteract the toxic illusion of self-judgment, I employ the concept of self-esteem, a temporarily useful fiction that replaces self-hatred for a while, helping me to make the transition to a deeper truth. Instead of an ego-based God who judges me unfavorably, I posit a more benign fiction: a benevolent God outside myself who loves me and would never cast me out. Beyond both fictions lies the reality: the oneness, or non-separation, of all Being. In seeing that I am not two, the notion of one entity judging another becomes eternally outmoded, and the myth dissolves with a divine smile.

⌒

Why do I sometimes find it difficult to apologize? My ego sees apology as an admission of a mistake, which the guilt-ridden mind equates with being permanently and incorrigibly bad. Apologies often sound insincere or defensive because the one who apologizes is holding back from seeing the full implications of his act. He fears that if he did see them, he'd feel unacceptably bad about himself. Freed from guilt, I live in a world where mistakes are allowed and comfortably acknowledged.

Why do I so frequently become uncomfortable in the presence of another's discomfort? Perhaps I suspect underneath that it's my fault they are unhappy.

The greatest help I can offer someone who feels bad about themselves is to be comfortable around their discomfort. However, this requires that I feel good about myself.

One of the greatest challenges to my ego is being unfairly blamed. Another is hearing myself disparaged in front of others. Responding with love seems impossible in such situations. My ego, outraged at the injustice, is overwhelmingly tempted to fight back, to defend myself with all the passion at my disposal. My response to these supposed injuries is an excellent barometer of my self-acceptance. The intensity of my defense is proportionate to my suspicion that I deserve the blame.

Why is it so painful to be rejected? The feeling of rejection is my ego's reaction when I put out what I think is love and someone doesn't receive it or respond in kind. In truth, my "rejection" is but an interpretation, a self-created fiction arising from guilt. I have given another the power to define my worth.

I offer love to my cat, she walks away indifferently, and yet I don't feel rejected. A young child is in a cranky mood and pushes me away when I try to hug him, so I honor him by leaving him alone for a while. When I offer pure love I don't hover around to make sure others receive it in just the way I want. I offer it with no strings attached; what they do with it is their business. Pure love is free of wanting anything from another; it takes no offense.

If I didn't reject myself, I wouldn't feel rejected.

I have many ways to avoid feeling the pain of my unworthiness, all of them unsuccessful:

- *I create ideals and try to live up to them.* Refusing to love myself unconditionally, I grudgingly allow a form of conditional love in which I set standards for myself. Should I live up to them, they render me temporarily adequate in my own eyes, until I raise the bar once more. These ideals may include the arenas of wealth, worldly power, success, reputation, intelligence, knowledge, physical attractiveness, or youth. I note that being seen as "spiritual" ranks highly among them.
- *I seek someone to love me unceasingly.* Doubting my worth, I bestow upon another the right and privilege to define it. As long as they smile upon me with unceasing approval, I temporarily relax my feeling of unworthiness. Yet I remain eternally vigilant for the moment when their love will flag, at which time I assume my traditional stance of guilt. This gives me just cause to resent them for the imperfection of their love.
- *I deny my own shortcomings.* Presented with overwhelming evidence of my inadequacy, I cover my eyes and ears in an

attempt to avoid perceiving what would clearly shame or embarrass me. By pretending the damning evidence isn't there, I delude myself into an artificial sense of adequacy.

• *I feel morally superior to others.* As a way to soften my suspicion of inferiority, I find a person or group toward whom I can feel superior. The worse I feel about myself, the more urgent my need becomes to pass judgment on others. As with other methods of avoiding guilt, the boost it gives to my ego never seems enough.

⁓

When I feel bad about myself, I'm parsimonious in my appreciation of others. I may, however, resort to flattery to entice others into giving me the love I crave. I may also experience embarrassment in receiving acknowledgment, since deep down I don't feel I deserve it.

When I form opinions about others, I decide first, unconsciously, how I am going to regard them, then I use their behavior as an excuse to see what I wanted to see. The same thing is true for myself. First I conclude that I am unworthy, for the ultimate offense of being; then I seek out particular actions, thoughts, and feelings that prove the validity of my primordial guilt. I conclude that I do not deserve love because I am self-centered, or have done something bad, or haven't lived up to my own standards of beauty, success, spirituality, perfection—whatever image my mind selects. After convincing myself that I am unworthy because of my particular behavior, I conclude that changing my behavior will render me acceptable. To attain this end, I envision an ideal that I must fulfill in order to deserve love.

.   .   .

Having standards of adequacy for myself implies that my love for myself is conditional. My attempt to feel adequate is based on the peculiar notion that love can only be deserved by good behavior. I try heroically to live up to my standards, unaware of the painful implication that I don't deserve love as I am, but must "earn" it. Since I am seldom able to live up to these ideals, I now have the perfect justification for harshness toward myself. In the event that I should occasionally succeed in attaining my standard, the bar is simply raised as I confront some new inadequacy. Whatever I do to prove that I am deserving, it is never quite enough. I am drinking salt water to quench my thirst.

I see how important it is to show myself compassion, and I intend to learn how. Toward that end, I become vigilant around the many ways in which I display my lack of self-compassion:

- Unloving thoughts about myself
- Harshness and judgment toward others
- Discomfort with other people's discomfort
- Defensiveness
- Ineffective boundaries: either closing my heart when I make one, or being wishy-washy
- Difficulty asking for what I want
- Attracting frequent negative circumstances to myself
- Self-sabotage
- Believing I don't deserve to feel good and creating a life where I don't
- Needing to be right
- Regretting the past

- Lacking confidence in myself
- Difficulty in making decisions, fear of wrong choices
- Feeling the need to lie or put on an act to disguise who I am
- Feeling easily insulted (which includes getting easily hurt or angry)
- Touchiness when criticized
- Feeling rejected
- Difficulty in apologizing or admitting mistakes
- Lack of ease in giving and/or receiving acknowledgment
- Giving my power to others
- Thinking that I know what another's path should be
- Being a perfectionist
- Ultimately, all relational difficulties

I do a friend a favor and am told how generous I have been. My ego refuses to accept the gift of acknowledgment, using typically twisted ego-logic: giving is supposed to be a sacrifice. In this situation I enjoyed giving, which means it wasn't real giving, and therefore didn't count. Of course, had I given out of obligation, feeling no joy, Ego would scold me for not doing it lovingly. There is no way Ego will allow me to give and feel good about myself. Come to think of it, there is no way Ego supports my feeling good about myself, period.

My self-judgment keeps me trapped in a cycle of deprivation. Out of my fundamental fear, I tighten, bracing myself more or less continually against the Universe's voluminous gifts. Feeling undernourished as a result, I turn to self-indulgence (say, in the form of food and drink) as a consolation. Disliking the uncomfortable consequences of this overindulgence, I am harsh with myself, which brings me back to the tightening that began the cycle. I am failing to appreciate the poignancy of the being who just wants to feel good and goes about it clumsily in the only way he knows how.

To prove my unworthiness, I set up contradictory standards for myself, which ensure that I cannot possibly earn my own approval. I condemn myself for not being honest with others, yet I believe my bluntness is offensive. I worry that I am an inadequate provider, but also that by pursuing material success I am compromising my ideals. I lack spontaneity, yet I blame myself equally for lacking discipline. However I behave, I find good reason to feel bad about it. Guilt always finds a way.

Guilt arises in part from my belief that if I were more loving, wise, disciplined, spiritual, and so on, things would go well for me. Since they haven't seemed to, the fault must be mine.

Someone speaks to me in a harsh tone and I find myself contracting, feeling more afraid. What am I afraid of? Whenever someone behaves this way toward me, it means they don't love me. If they don't love me, it means I am unlovable. If I am unlovable, it means I am rejected by God, unworthy of occupying space in this Universe. To some this worst of feelings is described by the concept of being a sinner. To others it is being a failure. But all of us caught up in the ego's dream partake more or less of this same, rather strange perspective.

⟜⟝

I may spend years attempting to improve myself morally and spiritually, yet I find that my ego has not become one iota nicer or less self-centered than it was at the beginning. This is not surprising—how can something "improve" when its roots lie in fearful illusion? Understanding this, I lose interest in trying to make my ego "better." Yet with greater awareness, Ego's self-hatred begins to soften, and its expression can become more skillful and conscious. Mind learns to dance more gracefully around Ego so that it creates fewer disturbances, inner and outer. In the presence of this greater harmony, it becomes easier to see that my ego is not who I am.

Self-judgment is Fear disguising itself as self-awareness.

One of the greatest of my fears is that of my own potential self-judgment, because, of all feelings, it is the hardest to live with. Guilt, or unworthiness, gives rise to more discomfort in my consciousness then everything else combined. Other negative feelings such as anger or sadness, purified of self-blame, move through to be released or transmuted. Guilt feels so uniquely awful because it arises from the insane assumption that I am so bad that I don't deserve to be. It is an aberration that, unlike other more natural feelings, has no redeeming value.

⌒

I feel uncomfortable with others to the extent that I believe I can't be myself with them. I believe I can't be myself in proportion to how much I think I will judge myself in their presence. Fear arises in the tension between "I want to be true to myself" and "I can't be myself because they would find me unacceptable." This tension persists as long as I feel unworthy.

Part of my discomfort in relationship comes from wanting something from the other, accompanied by the fear of not getting it. Another part comes from wanting something from myself. In order to suppress my core feeling of unworthiness, I demand of myself that I live up to the image Ego has created, which I hope will elicit the admiration or respect from others I believe I require to feel adequate. I demand from myself that I be wise, or witty, or charming, or successful, or interesting, or beautiful, or dominant, or humble, or spiritual, or "ordinary," and so on, so that I can feel good about myself. I set standards for myself, giving myself high grades if I can pull off a suitably impressive persona. This creates a dilemma. On the one hand, I try to behave in such a way as to win others' approval. On the other hand, being aware of trying to create a good impression, I feel bad about myself for the lack of integrity implied in the very act of doing that. Sometimes I hover over myself, waiting for a mistake so I can pounce. Who could be comfortable in such an inner environment?

Feeling bad about myself doesn't automatically imply that I must use others to make myself comfortable; but it does mean that I need to be very conscious to avoid doing that. A great deal of my social life is tiring or unrewarding because I put so much effort into living up to these standards, rather than simply being who I am.

Others' criticism of me is a mirror for my own self-dislike. It is useless trying to get them to stop criticizing me. It is more productive to get myself to stop criticizing me.

The projection of my self-judgment can manifest either as judgment of others for the same trait, or as the belief that they are judging me. Whenever I believe that I am experiencing someone else's ego, I am really experiencing my own ego disguised as another's. Since Ego is unreal, only Ego believes that it can see Ego. When I observe struggles in another, without Ego, I see them as essentially my own.

How often do I give another the power to define my worth! First I doubt my worth, and then I use the other's approval as a way of getting rid of that doubt. If their approval flags, I am in trouble; I take offense and resent them because they can never love me sufficiently. The more they love me, the more I hate them whenever there is the slightest interruption in their love, because it triggers my already-present feeling of unworthiness. Believing that they have caused me to feel guilty, I blame them for my pain.

I normally believe I dislike others for what they have done to me. However, it is quite possible to dislike another for what I do to them. I snap at someone unfairly for a mild transgression. Later I approach them to make up. As I come near I feel distant, cold, and, to be honest, a bit annoyed. But the annoyance is not over anything the other has said or done. It is because their presence triggers my guilt at having closed my heart. Being around them, having to "make up" to them, reminds me of my deep dislike of myself; I resent them for triggering this unfortunate feeling.

Perhaps all my defenses are ultimately against the ruthless voice of self-judgment.

Becoming defensive in response to criticism means that I'm afraid the other is right in implying that I am bad. Even though the presumed purpose of my defenses is to make myself feel safe, it never succeeds. In fact, the more defensive I am, the less safe I feel.

If I am accused of doing something foolish, insensitive, or unconscious, my defenses can assume various forms: "I had good reason to do that" (justification); "What do you mean? I never did such a thing" (denial); "I'm not listening to this" (withdrawal); "What you did is even worse!" (attack); "How can you say such a hurtful thing?" (emotional meltdown); "Oh, like you're perfect?" (sarcasm).

On the other hand, if I'm feeling good about myself, I feel no need for defense. My response might be, "Yes, I did do that. I was just thinking about myself and not about you at all. I guess I blew it. I see why that bothered you. I'm sorry."

The ego believes it requires denial to protect itself. Protect itself from what? Perhaps from apprehending the truth that would cause it to evaporate.

I see one of my friends who appears to be in denial, and become annoyed with him. Why is this? Denial is just one of the many expressions of fear, no better or worse than others. Could it be that when I judge someone in denial, I am looking into a mirror, failing to see the denial on the part of the judge?

If I am spiritually inclined, it is possible for me to become filled with anger and judgment yet be unwilling to acknowledge it because I wish so much not to be that way. To see the ego clearly in action requires an exquisite balance of unflinching honesty and compassion toward oneself. The challenge is to acknowledge one's imperfections without condemning them. Without honesty, denial triumphs; but the presence of self-judgment also inhibits self-knowledge, since full admission of Ego's unsavory feelings and thoughts may be too painful.

A similar denial of my imperfections arises from judging others. I see someone trying to impress others and judge them for it. I am too embarrassed to acknowledge this trait in myself. Possessing a self-image of one who never tries to impress others, I deny that reality in myself. I do so in order to avoid feeling the guilt entailed in being just like those I disparage. I seldom allow myself to admit an imperfection if I know I'm going to berate myself for having it.

Conversely, when I know I'm going to be gentle with myself for my failings, I allow myself to see them more readily. In so doing, do I risk being complacent about my flaws? Not really. The task is to replace denial with acceptance—not of the flaw, but of myself as a flawed person. "I accept the fact that I blame and resent for now, and I wish to stop." Beyond self-judgment lies the passion for freedom, out of which I urge myself lovingly toward greater awareness.

As I become more aware of Ego's nature, I begin to uncover its essential violence. Ego, underneath its various postures, wishes to destroy what it perceives as the not-self. Shock at another's behavior, or at my own inner landscape, entails denial of Ego's fundamental nature. The capacity to be shocked is an accurate measure of the gap between my ego's idealized image of itself and reality.

• • •

In asserting that my negative emotions such as anger and hurt are perfectly fine, I may glibly adhere to a kind of "spiritual correctness." I say that all this is "okay." Well, Yes, at one important level it is all okay. But if I really believed that, then I wouldn't have created all those negative feelings in the first place. Such feelings can only arise from the sense that things are not okay, which leads to resistance and its consequent negativity. Then, on top of that, I artificially superimpose the idea that everything is okay, which simply doesn't ring true.

⌒

Taking offense is a primordial gesture of a mind that feels bad about itself. As the mind learns to discharge its feeling of unworthiness, it also releases the need to feel insulted.

How often do I close down emotionally in the belief that it will keep me from being hurt? Is it really my openness that hurts me, or is it my taking offense?

If someone speaks to me crossly, I either react with insult or respond with compassion, depending on whether or not my ego is running my feelings. Most of the hurt and anger I experience stems from the feeling of being insulted. Yet investigation clearly shows that when I feel insulted, it is not something done to me by another, but something I do to myself.

Although it may not be apparent, feeling insulted is a choice. The very words "take offense" imply that I have decided to respond in a certain way. Since insult normally feels like something done to me, how do I come to see that it's my choice?

• • •

An opportunity is presented whenever I encounter unloving behavior in others. Since this happens often, I have many occasions to take offense. The choice to do so happens swiftly and mechanically: it is my default setting, my path of least resistance. In order to find another way, I need to locate the possibility of choosing not to be insulted, and to trust that it would feel better to make this choice.

The key lies in being alert the instant prior to taking offense. When a disparaging remark is made to me, I can learn—if I pay attention—to catch the beginning of feeling annoyed, frustrated, or physically tense. I become aware of this fact, while dwelling inwardly in a place where I can observe it with equanimity. My comfortable asylum of observation is crucial to my capacity to alter how I feel.

There are two things I wish to hold in balance. One the one hand, I accept my inner reality of this moment, the feeling of being offended. At the same time, my intent is to separate myself from this feeling. I dedicate my intelligence, heart, passion, and spirit to learning not to take offense. This has nothing to do with denying, repressing, or fighting against difficult feelings. It has more to do with observing what happens in my mind when I become offended.

I may get a better sense of the process by going back over it afterward in slow motion, to see the moment of choice. It's a little like playing a video game where enemies are firing missiles at me so rapidly that I have no time to dodge them. Suddenly I find a switch that slows down the speed. Now I see the missiles clearly and have plenty of time to catch them in midair or get out of the way. Slowing down time helps me develop an alert awareness of the instant I take offense. A clue is found if I can recall an instance when something "offensive" was said, yet, for whatever reason, I chose not to take offense. Through practice I become more adept at catching my negative reactions so early that releasing them is increasingly effortless. My attempts to observe myself over time bear fruit when one day I refuse to take offense at something I normally find "insulting."

In letting go of my feeling of being insulted, I understand that no outside source has hurt me. Here lies true forgiveness. Moreover, as I begin to see that I am no longer a victim of others' behavior, I possess a whole new mastery over my inner life.

Love and offense don't mix. If I love someone who is not interested in receiving my love, in understanding my difficulty, in sharing what interests me, or even in showing me respect, how much does it matter? To the extent that it does, I am probably feeling offended, because I am not getting what I wish in return for offering what I call my "love." But genuine love is not conditional; it asks nothing in return. It can be distressing to acknowledge that what I am offering isn't real love, because it shatters my image of myself as a loving being.

On discovering I have been lied to, I take offense, believing that the other lied with the purpose of hurting me in some way. If I understand that the real impulse behind lying is usually not an attempt to punish, but rather an effort to avoid the feeling of guilt, my sense of insult gives way to compassion. Further, if I become aware of how often I lie for such reasons myself (either through commission or omission), it is much harder to feel insulted.

What takes place when someone says or does something to imply that I don't deserve love? The mind interprets this as meaning that they have hurt me, assuming there is a something that can be hurt. It might be useful to ask "Who feels insulted?"

Pride (in the sense of that which can be wounded) is Ego's version of self-love. Ego confuses this pride with dignity.

Feeling comfortable with myself, I take no offense. Pride, which actually arises out of self-hatred, is what gets insulted. The greater the pride, the greater the tendency to take offense. Insult and pride are twin aspects of the same phenomenon.

I imagine myself as Christ, in the guise of a venerable and dig-nified black man in the old South. A white man speaks to me with contempt, using a racial epithet. As Christ, I can easily imagine feeling no insult, but rather compassion, for this fear-ful, misguided individual. What prevents my feeling that way now toward those who "insult" me?

The thought of anybody feeling superior to me triggers my pride. I wish to fight back, to show that they are wrong. But why should this annoy me unless I, too, think myself superior? If I am holding on to an image of myself as one who is beyond feeling superior, this may be a painful observation.

When someone I love is unloving toward me, I tend to feel bad. The question is: what, exactly, is going on? Pursuing that investigation leads swiftly to the heart of my feeling of unworthiness.

Someone appears to hate me. What is actually happening? One way to look at it is this: a deluded denizen of The Dream is having a fantasy of danger, and erects a meaningless defense by battling a symbol of what doesn't exist. Will I allow this to upset me? The choice is mine.

When I truly respect myself, the disrespect of another is seen clearly to be a statement about them rather than me. I may have made a mistake in my behavior toward them, but it's a mistake I needed to make, and I am still deserving of love. To find that love, I look within.

I don't trust another because I don't trust that I really wish them well. If I wish them well unreservedly, it's easy to imagine them feeling the same toward me. I tend to believe that other people feel toward me the way I regard them.

I encounter someone who seems not to like me, and I become uneasy. Normally in such situations, I both identify with my discomfort and try to escape it. My usual methods include: inwardly putting the other down; trying to be nice so they will like me; distracting myself with food and drink; becoming hostile; withdrawing and going numb. Suppose I do none of these. Suppose instead that I allow myself to feel my discomfort fully, but with compassion for my own pain. The discomfort may remain, but it is likely to soften. Underneath the surface, I may even start to feel comfortable with it. Once that happens, I may be more at ease with my behavior.

If I perceive self-judgment, it is useful to ask: is it just myself I blame, or do I condemn all who have this trait? I may find that I extend more understanding and forgiveness to others than I do toward myself.

Egos thrive on double standards. A young child can make as many mistakes as he needs to and I don't love him any less. However, I don't accord myself the same latitude: my sins are unforgivable. It seems that some who make mistakes deserve judgment and some don't; apparently I'm one of the ones who do. I ask myself, if I could love myself unconditionally, would I absolutely want to? In the hesitation that follows lies a profound opportunity for self-exploration.

Without this double standard, we are all equals. Either we all deserve condemnation for our sins, or we deserve love despite our imperfections. If my failings make me unworthy, the child's must prove the same about him. If he deserves love unconditionally, then it must be so with me as well. Which of these two possibilities feels more deeply in alignment with Truth? My Deeper Wisdom tells me where to take my stand.

Whenever I condemn myself for an imperfection, I can ask how I'd feel if someone I loved had the same shortcoming. If the answer is different, then I have employed a double standard. If I were sufficiently aware of it, I would have a harder time retaining my self-judgment.

A friend has serious trouble controlling his eating, and his weight balloons. Part of me loves it; it reminds me I'm not the only one with such struggles, which means I can feel a bit better about myself. But it is still easier to be understanding and gentle with my dear friend than with my own periodic inability to control the raging monster of appetite. Toward him I feel warmth, appreciation of his struggle, and unmitigated good wishes, without any need to "forgive." Surely this is the way I am meant to view my own struggles. Yet how much less kind is my view of myself! How much could it benefit from the quality of compassion with which I view my friend!

It's not so much making a mistake that I fear, but the harsh judgment I expect from myself in reaction. One of my most insane standards is that I should never make mistakes. The irony of holding to this painfully impossible ideal lies in the fact that I do so in the supposed interest of releasing my feeling of unworthiness . . . by being perfect. I don't sufficiently challenge this insanity. I could instead assert my intention to be especially gentle with myself when I make a mistake. Should there be any resistance to this, I am now in touch with the core of my difficulty.

The typical attitudes I take toward my mistakes include guilt, denial, and justification, the last two being an attempt to escape the first. They have in common the strange belief that I am bad because I make mistakes. Since mistakes are inevitable, it's not very smart to set it up so that I am guaranteed to hate myself. In fact, that in itself is quite a mistake.

Do I see some mistakes as acceptable and others not? Or are we all like children—learning to walk, falling down and skinning our knee? When I'm able to perceive all mistakes in that light, I don't differentiate between "good" and "bad" mistakes. Mistakes are permissible, and I wish to learn from mine.

I come upon a child who is too afraid to love, and I have compassion for him. I turn my attention inward toward a being who is also too afraid to love. What prevents that same compassion?

I can regard my mistakes in one of two ways. The first is that of the fire-and-brimstone preacher, who tells me that those who don't live up to correct spiritual standards will burn in Hell. The other is exemplified by the story of the poor sinner who approaches the Pearly Gates. Saint Peter greets him sternly, asking "Well, did you lead a righteous life and follow all the teachings?" The sinner looks down, ashamed, and confesses "No, to tell the truth I didn't." St Peter frowns for a moment, then breaks into a smile and says, "Ah, that's all right, come on in anyway!"

If I'm gentle with myself, am I saying that it's acceptable to me that I'm so unconscious? Not at all. Being kind to myself can include urging myself lovingly toward greater awareness. When I make a mistake, it's okay, and there is an opportunity for learning. If I don't take advantage of the opportunity, I become complacent. If the acceptance is missing, I am crippled by self-hatred. It can be a subtle pathway to move beyond the mechanical mind while being tender with myself for my failings.

⌒

Guilt feeds on itself through reflection. When I go through a long stretch of being emotionally closed down, I am likely caught in a vicious circle. I become aware that I am closed, which doesn't feel good. Wishing to be open and believing that I should be, I blame myself for being closed. Pushing against my state only serves to keep me locked in place. My contraction, resisted, has become a spasm.

A similar vicious circle may occur when someone criticizes me. My already-existing feeling of unworthiness increases, and I send back a subliminal message that proclaims that I don't deserve love. The other is quick to pick it up and believe it, the way a dog senses a fearful person or animal is worthy of attack. They blame me further, which exacerbates my guilt. Thus the cycle continues.

Nature is never stuck. The feeling of being stuck is traceable to the mind's vicious circles. Lovingly accepting my current state is a most practical way of becoming unstuck.

When I feel uncomfortable around someone, I naturally try to bolster my self-esteem. My two very different methods—both doomed to fail—are to get them to like me, and to judge them. Of course, when I judge them they will feel it and like me less. I will feel worse about myself, creating a nasty vicious circle.

Guilt is Ego's version of conscience. It is appropriate to have a moment of remorse when I become aware that I have done something unskillful or unconscious that brought pain. If remorse doesn't degenerate into guilt, it can transform into the intention to rectify the situation or change my behavior. Once I fully intend to take action, remorse has served its function and can be released.

If strong feelings of regret persist over a long time, I may suspect one of two things: either I haven't intended to take action, a sign that I'm not making use of a potential teaching; or else I am experiencing guilt, which is remorse infected with self-hatred. Unlike remorse, guilt leads to the perpetuation of the unwanted behavior. Feeling blamed by myself for my mistake, I am like a child with harsh parents, expressing his resentment by continuing the undesirable conduct. A child with loving and supportive parents would be more motivated to change the behavior. The same is true of the child in me. If I allow that child all the mistakes he needs to make, he will be more willing and likely to change.

Unworthiness is kept alive by the assumption that I deserve my harsh judgment. But in a moment of clarity I pause to examine this judge who, from quite an unloving stance, plays God, deciding who deserves love and who doesn't. Instead of believing in the judgment, I would do better to extend my compassion to the victim of his attack. And rather than becoming upset with the judge, I might consider extending him my compassion as well.

In this and every moment, I'm either indulging in self-judgment, or I'm allowing compassion to flow into myself. The way I was a moment ago has no meaning; I can be different this moment if I remember that I have that choice. Rather than poking through my history trying to find the source of my guilt, I would do better to dwell in my willingness to be kind to myself now. All the rest is just thought.

All my seemingly negative traits and actions arise out of some legitimate need, even if it is merely to ease my suffering a bit.

I would do well to be aware of that need before starting to judge myself. Instead of getting angry at my imperfections, I might dwell more profitably on what I want.

I find that I have often blamed myself for what I see as my numbness. Yet if I look back with understanding, I see that I adopted this numbness when I was young in order to avoid feeling unbearable pain. This was a totally appropriate response. Now I wish to experience my life force flowing vigorously, unimpeded by fear. If I dwell purely in that desire, my self-judgment converts to pure longing.

If my goal is to be self-loving, it makes no sense to employ a self-loathing means. Each moment, I have a fresh choice of either fighting against myself or embracing myself. When I seem unable to let go of guilt, I look within for the willingness to be kind to myself. This may include embracing the very being whose mechanism now includes the old habit of feeling unworthy. Dwelling in this embrace, I interrupt the ancient momentum of guilt. I find myself attracting people, teachings, circumstances, and insights that help move me in the direction of self-compassion.

One's greatest flaws and strongest virtues often turn out to be opposite sides of the same coin. The addict in me and the relentless drive toward freedom both arise from the strength of my discontent with the mind's prison. Instead of condemning the flawed side, why not just appreciate having the coin?

When I'm comfortable, I can give love to others. When I'm uncomfortable, I can give love to myself. Knowing that I can love myself, no matter what I am feeling, allows me to surrender more graciously to what is.

I work on forgiving myself by forgiving others; I work on forgiving others by forgiving myself.

⁓

My sense of "sin" from my past resembles the perception of light, whose intensity decreases with the square of the distance from the source. My perception of "sin" loses its intensity in proportion to how far it has receded in time. The same mistake feels worse by far if it happened yesterday than it will twenty years from now. How strange is the logic of the ego!

On the path to forgiving myself, I can perhaps make use of the fact that it is easier to forgive the younger me. How far back in history must I go before I can find compassion for myself? Can I imagine the three-year-old, sad and alone, and love him? I gaze at an old photo of myself—brooding, afflicted—and find that that one isn't hard. But doesn't that three-year-old live in me now? Doesn't he need my love? Perhaps I can manage to keep loving him as he gets gradually older, until finally I catch up fully with the present me.

I tend either to believe in my self-deprecating feelings or to bury them. Both strategies keep them alive. What allows these feelings to dissipate is to welcome them into the open air of awareness without believing in them.

Whenever I see something negative about myself, I have a choice: I can go either into the agony of self-judgment, or into gratitude that I've seen it and don't need to continue that way. Seeing everything that happens—externally and internally—as appropriate is a way of accepting what is. It's also a path toward self-compassion, because if everything has been appropriate, including my mistakes, where is the need for guilt?

There is nothing but arbitrariness in concluding that if I do well in the world, I'm worthy, but otherwise I am a failure. It has the same substance as my childhood belief that my favorite baseball team's winning or losing was cause for celebration or gloom.

My ego believes in gradations of worthiness, a notion at which my Loving Truth smiles.

$$\sim$$

When I am being self-critical, I try to recall the ways that have helped me move toward compassion for myself:

- I can believe that it's possible to love myself and develop intention and willingness to do so.
- I can develop a sensitive awareness toward all the secret, subtle ways I don't wish myself well, and learn to disbelieve them.
- I can be skeptical toward my self-condemnation. The knowledge of my basic goodness and divine connection lies underneath the feeling of unworthiness, and I can learn to find it.
- I can offer myself compassion especially in the midst of discomfort, or when I make a mistake.
- I can see that I am not bad for being presented with this particular lesson.
- I can look for thoughts that make me feel better.

- I can practice seeing others as worthy.
- I can view myself through the eyes of those who love and appreciate me.
- I can uncover my double standards of worthiness and challenge them.
- I can ask, in this moment, whether I am willing to be kind to myself.
- I can unhook my worth from "success" and appreciate the struggle. Love of myself is not something I have to earn.
- I can dwell on what I want instead of on what's wrong, appreciating that I'm just trying to ease my suffering.

~~~

If I wish to free myself of negative feelings, investigating the concept of "should" is indispensable. Whenever I am uncomfortable, lose my peace, or close my heart, there always seems to be a "should" lurking in the background. Living by these "shoulds" keeps me in conflict, out of touch with my true yearning. They are worth identifying so that I can pause and hold them to the light.

I come home after a long day, feeling bone-tired. However, I believe that I "shouldn't" be. Look at all the other people, I tell myself, who do so much more than I, yet have boundless energy. (Guilt loves comparisons.) In fact, my tiredness may simply be nature's call to encourage relaxation and allow the peace that heals. Without my "should," I might enjoy settling in and replenishing my reservoir. But my fatigue is unable to fulfill its purpose; being whipped by a "should," how could anyone relax? In fact, the friction created by the resistance of "should" rubbing against "is" may itself be a source of fatigue.

. . .

Since the "should" makes me upset and drained, what reason do I have for retaining it? My Deeper Wisdom can't locate a single advantage in holding on to this strange and deeply ingrained mental habit. Yet how often do I forget that the "should" is optional, something I myself impose on reality? If I could see that it has only the power I give it, I could release it and experience a lot more peace in my life. The only obstacle to that is the belief that the "should" is true and necessary. Is it possible to challenge that belief?

A dictionary definition of *should:* "an auxiliary used to express obligation, duty, propriety, necessity." The term "auxiliary" is telling; it denotes something added on to something else. What "should" adds on to is simply reality itself. Does reality need anything added? It is an interesting question.

"Should" can be thought of in two different ways. If I am facing north and want to go east, then I "should" turn right. This rightly implies that if I want something, certain behavior will help me attain my goal. But the second sense of the word opposes the reality of "what is" to an idealized state: "You should be more loving." This use of the term can carry all sorts of implications: for example, that if you don't behave lovingly, you are bad and don't deserve love yourself.

When I use the first "should," I need to be aware when what's wanted is unspoken and assumed. For example, "You should exercise and eat well" is really a shortened version of "If you want to be healthy, you should exercise and eat well." Assumptions like this are often some variation of "If you want Truth, Beauty, Goodness, Harmony, then you should . . ." Sometimes the unstated thought creates no problem; it is simply meant as a description of reality.

However, a statement beginning with "You should . . ." often carries the hidden assumption "If you want me to feel safe and adequate . . ." In other words, you should behave as I would wish so that I can release my discomfort. This in turn arises from the belief that I am not now safe or adequate, and I need you to be a certain way for me to feel comfortable. Since I need it, you "should" do it. Once held up to the light, the concept is rather difficult to support.

I say to you "You should always tell me the truth," which sounds plausible. But my real meaning is: if you want to please me by making me feel safe and adequate, you should always tell me the truth. The problem is, you may have priorities greater than trying to please me (you may also have good reason to suspect that telling me the truth may fail to please me). Asserting that your priority "should" be to please me is merely to substitute my own priority for yours. I end up saying to you, in essence, that you are bad if you don't make pleasing me your highest priority—a statement I would be embarrassed to make openly.

Sometimes I replace "You should . . ." with its close relative "I need you to. . . ." Both phrases make sense only when there is a specific goal in mind, confusion arising when the goal is unclear or unstated. "I need you to be monogamous," without the "in order to," is false; without your monogamy, I'm still here and breathing, which shows that I didn't really "need" it. On the other hand, if I add the unstated goal, the statement can be true: "In order for me to want to stay married to you, I need you to be monogamous." This makes perfect sense.

It might be tempting to conclude that I "shouldn't" have "shoulds." However, if "shoulds" and "shouldn'ts" are a mistake, I wish to avoid employing that very mistake in order to correct it. I prefer merely to notice that most "shoulds" with hidden agendas are untrue and are responsible for much suffering.

To relate to another person from a feeling of obligation is a classic example of Fear donning the mask of Love. Acting out of "shoulds" in the name of love generally benefits neither oneself nor the other person. If I am sick, do I want someone to spend time with me only because they think they ought to?

When I act out of obligation, I disrespect my own integrity. I discard my freedom to act as I see fit, and in so doing encourage myself to feel like a victim. As motivation, "should" is a poor substitute for healthy passion. The belief that I need obligation to supply the motive for my actions arises from the conviction that I am not worthy to follow my deepest inner guidance.

I come home tired and face a sink full of dishes. My partner says she has had a tough day and is exhausted. My first thought is: I don't feel like doing the dishes. To say I'd rather not, but "should" do the dishes, and then to do them grudgingly, means I'm not taking responsibility for my choice. When I act out of such "shoulds," I often carry resentment.

·   ·   ·

Although giving because I feel I "should" doesn't feel right, neither does automatically holding back. My other option is to get in touch with my love, which includes self-love. If a relationship is reasonably healthy, I usually wish my partner well, which means there will be a natural desire to give some of the time without the pressure of "should." My Deeper Wisdom takes into account the relative strength of my partner's needs and my own. When I act out of love, there is no formula: Sometimes I realize that I'm really tired and choose not to do the dishes. Other times I'm aware that my partner has had an exhausting day, and will love waking up and seeing a clean kitchen; I do the dishes because I want to. In both cases, I take responsibility for my choice: I do it because I want to, or don't do it because I don't want to. This frees me from the tension of feeling the obligation to give. By releasing the "should" and allowing myself to be moved by love, I retain my integrity, I feel no guilt, and my partner experiences my gifts as genuine.

Preference is a given in our dualistic universe. We all have preferences, and nothing will change that. But using the language of "should" often distorts and misrepresents those preferences in a problematic way. For example, instead of "I prefer that you show up on time," I say "You should show up on time." The former is a simple statement of fact about my feelings. The latter depicts you as the source of my upset whenever you don't.

Whenever I am uncomfortable, I am apt to make myself feel still worse by believing that I know what I "should" be feeling. Feeling my own lack of love or contentment, I cling to the belief that I "should" be comfortable, happy, disciplined, healthy, successful, spiritual, and so on. As a result of this merciless condemnation of my own discomfort, I feel bad about feeling bad. I have turned a minor contraction into a prolonged spasm.

I attend a social gathering where I feel awkward and out of place. The experience would be tolerable were I simply to acknowledge my discomfort. But believing that I should be enjoying myself creates a much deeper distress. The strength of my "should" is the measure of my resistance, and thus of my added discomfort.

I remark to a friend that a certain mutual acquaintance "should" have spent his inheritance more wisely. My friend asks me what I mean by that. I defend my judgment by saying that I believe this fellow would have been happier had he done it a different way. First of all, I most assuredly can't know that to be true. But more importantly, I feel I know better than he; I am enjoying the idea that my judgment is superior. In other words, I am closing my heart to someone in the guise of claiming to wish them greater happiness.

This dynamic often infects the process of giving advice to others. If I believe somebody should be behaving differently, my heart is generally closed to them. All I will offer is disapproval, condescension, and a sense of non-safety. A little honesty shows me that this sets up a barrier and fails to change anyone's mind. Others respond not to the content of what I am saying, but to the presence or absence of love in my expression. Only through feeling accepted in their being will they let me in.

.   .   .

I attend a public event where some people are acting loudly and inappropriately. I allow myself to be bothered, believing that they ought to obey the rules and be more considerate of others. My nervous system is perhaps slightly jarred by their rowdiness. However, this accounts for about one percent of my discomfort. The other ninety-nine percent comes from my judgment that they "shouldn't" behave that way. Is that judgment true? And does it serve me to make it?

It's easy to believe that people "shouldn't" act to inconvenience me. It's especially easy when I decide that they are emotionally immature. But one of the hallmarks of people behaving immaturely is that they don't take responsibility for their actions. They flail around and create havoc, unaware of the effect they have on others. But is this any different from an actual child? A child is not aware that others are affected when they yell or have a tantrum. Once I see that someone is capable of behaving childishly, doesn't it seem strange to apply a severe judgment each time they exhibit this behavior? Do I think that a dog shouldn't bark because his bark is annoying me? Dogs bark. Children act like children. And people act like people, which is to say that they often act immaturely. I have much occasion to observe myself doing the same. That's what we humans do; it's our nature.

If I search for it, I can find much thoughtlessness and self-centeredness in the world. Walking through my life grimacing when I encounter loud children, barking dogs, people acting immaturely, criminals, dishonest politicians, exploiters of the environment, and so on, I can easily find excuses every day to cut myself off from the universal source of well-being. Does my

suffering, my annoyance, my judgment contribute to the
world's improvement? I think not. Being afraid for humanity is
in the same category as being afraid for my individual life. I can
view the future of this planet in exactly the same way as I view
the future of this body: either with or without fear.

Does this mean that I support inappropriate behavior? Not at
all. It's just that my "shoulds" create discord in me. This discord
expresses itself as righteousness and blame, which is felt by
others and limits my influence on them. Shedding my judgments increases my capacity to act positively. I don't have to be
upset to take skillful action, to make boundaries, to express
myself. If my purpose is to communicate, I would have a better chance of success through releasing my "shoulds" and
approaching those who annoy me with an open heart.

Regret is largely a belief that something should or shouldn't
have happened. I feel I acted wrongly, or others acted wrongly
toward me. I contemplate the painful events from my past and
wish they had never occurred. All this implies that I possess the
precise knowledge of how events should unfold on my journey. Do I really know what the particular rhythm of my own
awakening should be? Wishing that something had not happened is a form of arrogance; I assume a God-like role in
knowing what is ultimately good or bad on my own or
another's path of learning.

My behavior is often the result of contrary impulses. The force
that predominates determines the action. I blame myself
because one force predominated over another, as if this were
reprehensible. For example, one side of me wants to lose

weight, and another wants to continue eating as much as I feel like in the moment. I identify myself with the part that wants to change, refusing to acknowledge that the part unwilling to change may currently be stronger. When I blame myself under such circumstances, I might usefully ask who or what I am blaming. An impulse? Once I release the belief that I know how things should be, a major stronghold of my ego crumbles for lack of foundation.

In watching a play, I accept that all the characters need to act out their roles, virtuous or otherwise. Does it help to regard real life as a "play"? The two kinds of "play" have in common the fact that I have no control over the action on stage, only over my response. I'm often upset in the real-life "play" because of my belief that many of the characters should be different from the ones they actually are. Is this belief helpful? What if I had the same attitude to the characters in this play of life as I do toward the characters in a real play, where the villain needs to behave as a villain? Perhaps I would walk through my own role a lot less upset and with more grace.

My ego claims, "I don't like releasing 'shoulds.' Without 'shoulds,' I would fall apart; I need moral principles to act appropriately and to accomplish something in my life. Obligations are what keep us all from descending into chaos."

A friend, having trouble with the concept that "shoulds" are unnecessary, says to me, "I am absolutely certain that people shouldn't leave loaded guns where kids can get at them. Nothing feels more obvious. How can you or anyone contradict that?" At one level, this does have a ring of truth. He is saying that out of our love of humanity, we want the world to be a kind place, free of ugliness and violence. If someone wants that, he will demonstrate it by being nonviolent, respectful, and—beyond a doubt—careful of children's lives. We might even want to prohibit leaving loaded guns around by law, if we think that will make our children safer. But what if someone violates these rules? What if someone is careless or impulsive, at that moment more interested in their own convenience than in a harmonious and safe world? What is the point of my demanding that others follow my rules and priorities? Of demanding, in other words, that they be different from the way they are? That demand will not make the world a safer or more harmonious place.

I live in a world of duality, where there exist kindness and unkindness, love and hate, joy and suffering. The idea of "should" impotently opposes this simple reality. Indeed, the concept contains an inherent contradiction. Whenever I impose my "should" on others, I judge them. But when I look at myself in the act of judging, what do I see? I see myself closing my heart, becoming upset, and projecting negativity—in short, demonstrating the opposite of what I believe others should exhibit. If I think being kind to others is a good idea, the way I'll express that is to be kind to others. Passing judgment on them isn't being kind.

Making other people's morality my business is not a way to improve the world. In fact, history teaches me that it is more a recipe for catastrophe than for the world's betterment. If, on the other hand, I simply exemplify the quality I wish others had, I wouldn't find their lapses such a problem. If the concept of "should" has any meaning for me, it is this: if I desire a peaceful world, I "should" demonstrate the kindness that, were it universal, would bring it about.

V

RELATIONSHIP

A fully ripened intimacy is the greatest of treasures. Yet the skill entailed in attaining it is hard-won, and the persistent work required is surely not what was bargained for at the beginning. It is easy in our culture to be deceived by the myth of the early romantic stage extended forever.

If this work is so difficult, what is my incentive for doing it? Isn't it the actual possibility of happiness? With dedication and persistence, I can make myself proficient in any number of areas and attain all kinds of success in the world. Seldom is this a road to happiness. But there is one activity virtually guaranteed to make me happy: learning to love another person.

Why is relationship such an important branch of any spiritual path? Because it's the place where I see either my love or lack of love most clearly manifested. It's the place where any tendency of mine toward denial or unconsciousness will be swiftly and unavoidably held before me. Observing myself with honesty in relationship will quickly dispel any fanciful image I may have of myself. It is my most powerful instruction in humility.

A tenet for spiritual relationship:

• What is pleasant, celebrate.
• What is unpleasant, investigate.

It's easy to conclude that happy long-term relationships are impossibly difficult or only for the lucky few. Of course, such an attitude is self-fulfilling. Believing in the possibility for one-self of a thriving, fulfilling, passionate intimacy is a precursor to having one. If one had such a vision, yearned for it with their whole being, and had confidence that they deserved it, barriers would crumble. My major barriers are my deeply embedded inner habits, so hidden and elusive that they seem part of me.

One pitfall is when I use the relationship in order to get some-thing from my partner: I try to get them to love me or be turned on by me. To make the right impression, I bend myself out of shape, losing my integrity and self-respect in the process. When this fails to work, I resent them for not giving me what I want. My resentment displays itself as a basic disre-spect toward my partner, which I justify as acceptable behav-ior. How can intimacy flourish in such an environment?

Another kind of obstacle results from my limited conception of the nature of intimacy. True connection with another involves more than intellectual, physical, or emotional content. By focusing mostly on content, I avoid the heart of intimacy, which is a conscious energetic connection in the moment, free of past images. Part of the beauty of a long-term relationship can be uncovering and releasing these obstacles, which only mask the true essence of relationship.

My strength and comfort in a relationship comes from only one place: that of self-acceptance. My fear of intimacy is especially intense when I feel unworthy. I then worry that others will see directly into my being and recoil in horror. I fear feeling rejected because I reject myself.

Perhaps I am afraid to expose the difficulties in my intimate relationship because it might lead to the relationship ending. True, it might. But what is my alternative? If I'm honest, I will contemplate what the rest of my life will be like if I do not take this risk: bickering continually, withdrawing sullenly, or persisting in a bland and depressing gray nothingness—an imitation of intimacy. Sensing the utter death in that inspires me with the courage to step into the unknown.

My fear of intimacy often expresses itself in a wish to avoid contact, to check out. My need for solitude can be perfectly healthy, but when it is prompted by unconscious avoidance, it does not serve me. I can find many ways to check out: being distracted or tired, finding extraneous things to do, drugs, food, TV. When I'm in such a place, I tend to function entirely from habit, saying things that might even sound intelligent but have been repeated countless times, telling the same stories, having the same conversations, expressing the same opinions. Too often, I take my daily bath in yesterday's bathwater.

The study of psychology, as well as common sense, tells me that anger is a perfectly normal human emotion, the presence of which is natural and healthy. My Deeper Wisdom tells me that although this is indeed true, the emotion usually arises from a false perception: I believe that I am threatened when I am not. Since my anger, as I usually express it, feels bad both to me and to whoever is receiving it, I have an interest in releasing this false perception at its source.

If anger is such a normal and healthy aspect of my emotional makeup, why does it usually feel so distorted and unpleasant when I feel and express it? With most anger, the heart closes and blame erupts. No unloving state can feel good; this kind of anger, intense in its non-loving, is particularly uncomfortable. On the other hand, when my anger is an expression of self-love, a boundary made with firmness and conviction but without blame, the anger feels invigorating and healthy. Because my heart has remained open, it has a deep comfort. The true function of anger is for self-compassion to make an effective boundary when a gentle boundary isn't heeded.

Anger can also serve a valuable function when I realize that I am sick of living as a slave to my mechanical ego, and I decide to change that. Anger then becomes a loud "No" to the stale, pain-producing habits of mind that perpetuate my suffering. It transmutes into the passion of divine discontent, supplying a powerful intention to go beyond my limitations.

When anger isn't released, it festers and accumulates over time as resentment. Resentment is usually unconscious; it pollutes the atmosphere with anger, often expressed indirectly. When I have accumulated a sufficient level of this toxin, its manifesta-

tions can play havoc with my intimacy. I may become frequently annoyed by what my partner does or says, notice their
flaws more than their virtues. I have difficulty forgiving them
their mistakes. My buried anger can erupt in the form of a
harsh tone or frequently picking fights. It may go in the other
direction, expressing itself as a dead tone of voice, lack of
energy, an emotional or sexual withdrawal. Or I may find reasons not to be with my partner, checking out when I am with
them, or finding myself with nothing to say. A sense of freedom or relief when they are gone may indicate that I believe
I can't be myself in their presence. Or it might mean that I
resent them more than I'm willing to admit.

To release these toxic feelings, I purify them by learning to
express my anger simply and cleanly, stripped of blame or justification. Anger expressed without attack is simply a kind of
growl that expresses my feeling. The growl of direct anger may
not ultimately be the most gracious of attitudes. It is certainly
not my last word. But on the way to transcending my anger, it
represents an improvement, leading to a swifter release of negativity and a cleansing of the relationship's dark underside.

I am easily capable of disguising my anger as love. I may tell
myself that I am being courteous or kind toward another
when I am actually conveying something quite different.
When my love is pure, it knows how to express itself in a way
that takes another's sensitivities into account in a way that
feels good to them. When my behavior offends, it means I
probably knew, at least at an unconscious level, that what I
had to say would be hurtful, yet chose to say it anyway. It is
hard to admit that such is my purpose. Yet if someone is not
responding well to what I believe are expressions of love,

chances are good that they are reacting to the resentment lurking beneath my good intentions.

My anger often arises from a mix of desire with frustration. I am conscious of strongly wanting something; but instead of focusing on getting it, I fixate on the fact that I'm not getting it. I believe myself powerless and become angry.

As I become more conscious, I learn to deal with my anger in more productive ways. At the least conscious stage, I tend to simply lash out at others with blame and judgment whenever I am angry, or else smolder with sullenness out of fear of being direct. At the next stage, I see how harmful this is to my relationships. I develop an ideal of not being angry, an ideal of understanding and forgiveness. In my effort to live up to this ideal, I often refuse to acknowledge my anger, which festers. Then I begin to see the unhealthiness of that. I learn to express my anger in a responsible and conscious way, cleanly and without judgment. This is as far as many of us are willing to venture.

Yet there is one more stage to the process: that of transmuting my anger through investigation. When I truly understand the source of my closed-hearted anger, when I see the mistaken beliefs that underlie it, then I understand that nobody else can cause me to suffer. Without the belief that another has caused my pain, I have no more reason to be resentful. My anger dies spontaneously.

I may have difficulty admitting that my explosive anger might be hard to be around, for fear I am admitting that I am bad. I may resist releasing blame for my partner's explosive anger for fear it means approving of that trait. In both cases, my blame around anger distorts my perception of reality.

Although my feelings of anger are natural and their occurrence unavoidable in the normal course of things, my mind has the power to turn them into something unhealthy. Upon first arising, my anger is quite authentic and spontaneous. After a brief period, it would naturally die down. However, my mind, with its obsessive thought, chews over the situation and continually recreates the anger, keeping it alive. The original anger, a genuine emotion, feels natural; however, its thought-created extension hardens into an aberration, uncomfortable and riddled with blame. Here is where my anger becomes an unhealthy indulgence. It is a source of unnecessary suffering well worth investigating.

Although there is value in simply remaining quietly with the energy of pure anger, once my self-justifying thoughts have whipped my anger up into a steady state of resentment and blame, then I am no longer "being" with the feeling. The same thing can be said of sadness. When thought chews on it obsessively, it becomes self-pity: self-pity is to sadness what blame is to anger. Both self-pity and blame are unnecessary intrusions of the mind onto a pure feeling. Both encourage me to perceive myself as powerless. I can do better.

Do I really wish to release my held anger? If I did so without ambivalence, it would already be gone. I may be more in touch with the part of me that wants to let it go; yet, because it's still there, I sense another part that prefers to hold on. What is this desire to stay angry? What advantage does my ego see in holding on to anger? What sacrifice do I believe I would be making if I let it go? Without my attachment to resentment, the natural anger of the moment would swiftly subside. It therefore behooves me to investigate the nature of this attachment.

In a moment of extreme provocation, I blast another person with ugly, violent anger, the kind I am later ashamed of. I am able to do this only if I consider such disrespect toward another acceptable. Once I have taken my stand that it is not, such behavior evaporates. It becomes the place where I draw the line, just as I would draw the line at killing someone. The motivation to take such a stand can occur in one second of insight.

As long as resentment is present, I live in Hell. As I ripen, I wish to become completely free of its tyranny. I would not aspire, nor would it be realistic to aspire, to eliminate perfectly natural bursts of anger on occasions. But there is a difference between this and resentment. Resentment is to momentary anger what a cramp is to a natural muscular contraction. A cramp is a muscular seizure lasting in time. Unlike a normal contraction, it does no useful work, but rather stays locked in place after the work is done. Resentment is an emotional cramp; it serves only to drain my energy. Self-interest dictates that I do everything in my power to clean out the underside of my relationships by releasing resentment. My goal is not to be without anger; I simply wish not to hold on to it.

Much of my anger arises from a belief that the Universe is a place of scarcity. Since there aren't enough goodies to go around, I must struggle to get my share of them. I rage against those who I believe stand in my way, as though they are keeping me from being happy. This is life seen as a game of musical chairs. The idea that the loving Universe is capable of providing us all with what we need feels viscerally superior to this dark picture of competition and scarcity. Once again, Truth feels better than illusion.

~

Why do I often resent my intimate partner more than anyone else? It has to do with my expectations, with how important their loving me is to my ego. Having doubts about my worthiness, I attempt to allay them by finding a partner who loves me unceasingly. If I am used to their love, I may come to depend on it for my sense of self-worth. They can't possibly fulfill this assignment: when they are tired, cranky, or fearful, their sun is covered by clouds and their love cannot shine through. If I'm not feeling their love, I conclude that they don't love me. If they don't love me, it proves that I am unlovable, which I suspected all along.

My resentment depends on my belief that my partner's insufficient love is a central cause of my suffering. If I assume that I need their love to be happy, then I am addicted to their love and a victim of their emotional state. They are the puppeteer and I am the puppet.

I may believe that I resent my partner because of their flaws, such as drinking too much, unskillful parenting, or spending too much money. However, if my partner retained these flaws but showed me daily love, kindness, and respect, would I still carry my heavy load of resentment? I think not. Ultimately my resentment arises from a fundamental source: I believe they haven't loved me consistently and well enough. This resentment then seeks out flaws, which usually aren't hard to find. Then I delude myself into thinking their specific flaws are what have provoked me, rather than my global resentment that is seeking something to blame.

Because I conclude that my partner is making me suffer, I hate them and want them to suffer equally. If, just before I said something that hurt my partner, I stopped to consider the effect it would have on them, I would probably admit that what I was about to say would be hurtful. And with a bit more honesty, I would see that that was indeed my intention: my ego wants to punish them for having hurt me. How distasteful!

One of the most effective ways to punish someone is to make them feel guilt, the most unpleasant of all feelings, by reminding them continually of how much they have hurt me. I do this by holding back my own love. I want them to hate themselves as much as I hate them. In their feeling bad, I feel a perverse enjoyment, a kind of consolation prize replacing real love. I am now in the special Hell that couples inhabit when their hearts are closed.

In truth, my pain arises not from another's lack of love, but from my belief that they are wise in not loving me. I adopt the bizarre stance of wishing others to disagree with my evaluation of myself.

~

I feel something missing in my relationship because I'm not being met at a deep level. The question is, am I offering unconditional love and not being met? Or am I merely withholding love and getting back a similar energy? The two have a totally different flavor. The partner I would encounter if I offered perfect love (or even a semblance of it) would be so different from the one who reacts to my holding back that I have no capacity to evaluate the relationship accurately until I first make that shift. Once they begin to feel my unflagging love, something in them melts. Invariably, over time, they become a different person.

My partner says No to what feels like a reasonable request. I feel hurt and righteous. Why do they do this to me, I wonder, when I always give them what they ask for? Then I remember to take a breath, soften for a moment, and ask myself whether this is really true. When my partner desires my love or attention, do I always want to give it to them? The answer, I have to admit, is no. I realize that when I am ungiving to my partner, they must have the same response to it as I do. Is there a double standard here?

Instead of blaming my partner, I need to be aware that we both sometimes allow fear to close us down, causing discomfort all around. I need to inhibit the mechanism that automatically turns discomfort into blame. I look instead for the willingness to transcend the Hell into which I have placed myself. Because I am no longer feeling morally superior, healing isn't far off.

My partner's very unhappiness, which is not much different from my own, gives me still more reason to think worse of myself; I believe that if I were a better partner, they would be happy all the time. This is perhaps why I often resent the one

I love, simply for being unhappy or ill. I fail to see how actually unloving is the covert demand that one's partner be always healthy and happy.

I go to sleep angry with my partner. Awakening in the morning, I feel fine, until I suddenly recall my mood of the previous night. At this point, I observe myself picking up my anger again. "Let's see, where was I?" I say. Ego is caught in its typical strategy of perpetuating pain.

When my partner is upset with me, I can disguise my reactive anger as caring. For example I say "I'm sorry you feel that way," implying "end of subject." Although it superficially resembles sympathy, my response elicits annoyance. The fact that it does might make me suspicious of my motive. In truth, I am implying that I had nothing to do with my partner's upset. I can also declare, argumentatively, "Look, I didn't *mean* to hurt you!" Such a response often triggers further anger; it comes across as a justification for behaving insensitively. Furthermore, if I am truly moved by compassion for my partner, then what I did or didn't "mean" is, at bottom, irrelevant.

⌐∽

I wish to have healthy boundaries, ones that are both firm and loving. An indication that I do have them is when I feel equal comfort in responding to another's request with either Yes or No. Discomfort in saying Yes (harsh boundaries) arises from resentment. The other feels disrespected, and resentment increases between us. If I have discomfort in saying No (weak boundaries), I give the other person power over me and resent them for that.

·   ·   ·

Without comfortable boundaries, I am like a declawed cat entering the woods, understandably afraid because other creatures now have an unnatural power over me. I may walk through life with the limited relational goal of merely avoiding the upset of others. Fortunately, this declawing is reversible. Functional claws arise from being in touch with what doesn't feel right, and having the self-compassion and courage to say no!

If I have weak boundaries, then I may want to examine more precisely what is entailed in making good ones. First, I need to develop the habit of asking myself more frequently what I want in the moment, positively or negatively. To find the true answer, I then need to sink down beneath my attempts to "figure out" my judgments and "shoulds" and get in touch with my deeper truth. Once this is ascertained, I need to be willing to express my wishes directly, asking clearly for what I want and making firm boundaries around what I don't.

When good boundaries are lacking, it is useful to find out where in this process the difficulty lies. If, lacking self-love, I habitually try to please, I may blind myself to the very existence of my own honest likes and dislikes. Because I am so used to doing what the other wants, I abandon the normal and healthy habit of consulting my own desires, until their very existence no longer occurs to me.

Should I manage to transcend this habit, other difficulties await me. Over time, my conditioned mental judgments may have blocked the instinctive capacity to identify my own deepest wishes. If my mind is filled with a confusing array of "shoulds," I may have difficulty getting in touch with my true preference. Finally, even if I do come to know well what I do or don't want, I may not express myself clearly and firmly for fear of causing displeasure in another. If my self-esteem is shaky, this may feel like the ultimate catastrophe, a hopeless conflict. Going beyond these obstacles will allow me to feel a new strength in my relationships.

Why do I find it difficult to make boundaries? My discomfort with it is traceable to my lack of self-worth. I may tell myself that I'm uncomfortable because someone will get angry or stop loving me. In truth, I am not afraid of their response, but rather of how I believe it will make me feel. If in setting a boundary I feel good about myself, then it won't much matter if the other person doesn't like where it is placed (think of a loving and skillful parent responding to a cranky child). I will be upset by their negative response in proportion to the guilt I feel in making the boundary.

⌒

There is a gradation in how tolerable my partner's shortcomings can seem, depending on how I view them. At the first level, I see clearly that the problems are all the result of my psychological baggage, having really nothing to do with my partner. At the second, I see my partner's imperfections, recognize that they are aware of them and working to change, and decide that I can live with that. At the third, I acknowledge that their imperfections are not likely to change, or that they are not sufficiently motivated to change them; yet I still feel that I can live with that. The fourth and final level is deciding that I cannot tolerate their shortcomings, and that if they do not change I can no longer remain in the relationship. There is often confusion among these, and it is well to be clear which one represents my deepest Truth.

⁓

I am with a friend who is going on and on about his problems. I become restless and begin to feel resentful. Feeing "trapped" by his talking, I explore this familiar feeling. It's easy to forget that I choose what I do, where I go, with whom I associate.

The feeling of being trapped can only arise when I don't have a firm commitment to honor myself. If I honored myself and still found myself in an untenable situation, I would know that I would do everything conceivable in my power to act on my own behalf and remove myself from that situation. With myself as my greatest ally, I can't imagine feeling trapped.

What is my motive in listening to someone when I'm bored? I may listen because I believe that's what a friend should do, or because I fear that making a boundary will lead to my being disliked. Such motives lead to victimhood and resentment. However, if they are sharing something that truly interests them, I may listen as a loving gift to them. When listening occurs out of love, it has another flavor and leads to different results. If I am truly interested in another person, then I am more capable of encouraging a meaningful, intimate conversation. If they are being boring because they themselves aren't that interested, I can gently suggest as much. And if they do go on too long, Love will know how to handle it graciously. Love knows quite well when and how to end the conversation swiftly with a minimum of conflict or offense.

·   ·   ·

A friend complains to me about another friend of mine. It makes me slightly uncomfortable. What are my alternatives? I can listen stoically, resenting the complainer and feeling like a victim. I can join with their ego and justify them in blaming the friend. Or I can impatiently blurt out "I don't want to hear about it." But when my boundaries are healthy and balanced, there are better choices. One might be to say to myself "I chose to be here. They need to let off steam, and it does me no harm. I'll make use of this occasion to practice extending my love." I might validate their feeling without encouraging blame: "I see why you might be mad at so-and-so," rather than "Yes, that's outrageous." Or I might realize that this isn't working for me, and that I need to make a loving boundary. Then I might say to my friend "I understand how you must be feeling; but in this case, since we're talking about so-and-so, it's a little hard for me to hear. If he were talking about you, I would feel the same."

⌒

If I lack comfortable boundaries, I may believe that showing love to my partner would result in an overwhelming demand for more. For example, even though I would enjoy receiving loving touch, I may nonetheless avoid it, because I fear making a boundary if the situation goes farther than I am ready for. Rather than avoiding physical affection altogether, I am better off learning to set limits graciously.

My lack of good boundaries is related to my failure to ask for what I want. Both arise from my fear of clearly communicated preferences. Both bring me to a place of resentment.

·   ·   ·

What prevents me from asking for what I want? Do I fear not getting it? Am I afraid that asking will cause a disturbance? If I've been resenting my partner for not giving it to me, perhaps I think that if they do, I'll have to stop blaming them. Underlying my reluctance is often the conscious or unconscious belief that I don't deserve what I'm asking for. These are all manifestations of fear, which it behooves me to examine.

I may believe, when I am hesitant to ask for something, that I fear the other person's "No." In truth, it's not the "No" in itself that triggers my fear, but the "No" as I interpret it. If I treat refusal as a personal rejection, then I feel trapped. By asking, I risk rejection; by not asking, I risk not getting and the subsequent resentment. Both risks come from within me. My sense of rejection would be impossible were I not rejecting myself. And my resentment is based on my belief that my well-being is dependent on getting what I ask for. If I thought that it would be nice to have something but knew I would be fine without it, I'd have no fear of not obtaining it and could ask easily. If I could, I'd probably get satisfaction more often.

The fear of asking for what I want is related to my fear of offering love. In both cases, I am paralyzed by my fear of being rejected.

I may dismiss or condemn others' behavior as being "needy." But am I not being needy any time I depend on my partner's disposition for my own sense of well-being? If I look honestly, I notice that whenever my partner is in a bad mood, I feel slightly resentful. How hard this is to admit, how unspiritual!

· · ·

When I'm feeling bad about myself, I may attempt to disgorge this disagreeable feeling by trying to obtain my partner's non-stop love and approval. In such a state of need, I am unable to relax. I closely scrutinize how my partner is responding, modifying my behavior as I go so as to maximize their approval. Yet whenever I seek this approval, my partner always perceives my intentions at some level. This tends to turn them off, increasing my neediness. In making my demands, I am asking for something that I, myself, am incapable of giving. Worse, I am reinforcing the fiction that another person has both the capacity and the duty to make me happy. Looking to receive my sense of adequacy and wholeness from my partner's love is a strategy that can never succeed.

To break out of this vicious cycle requires that I identify the needy feeling as it is happening. It rarely comes in a loud voice that says "You're being needy!" But I can learn to recognize the familiar flavor of weakness and frustration at not being sufficiently loved or understood. The feeling is intensified because I don't like myself for feeling that way. I despise myself for the way I subtly persist in asking for affection and understanding; how abject it seems. Sometimes my neediness masquerades as Love by thrusting "loving" behavior at my partner with the clear message that it had better be returned, together with the implied threat that if it is not, I will sink (with total justification, of course) into self-pity or resentment.

My neediness is really a matter of wanting to use my partner to convince me of my own safety. My desire to feel safe is legitimate; I've just been looking in the wrong place.

· · ·

Is it reasonable, when I am feeling vulnerable and needy, like a child, to expect my partner to offer loving help? It is natural in that state to *want* emotional nourishment, and fine to ask. But is it appropriate to *demand* it? For one thing, my partner may be unable or unwilling to offer help at that moment, something I am powerless to change and foolish to judge. For, in all honesty, do I respond lovingly to all of their needs? A better approach might be to ask without demanding. If my partner can offer help, fine. If not, I can perhaps go to a friend for sustenance; or, ultimately, I can go within.

When the pain of neediness becomes too great, I may attempt to deny it by pretending not to care: "The hell with you, I don't need you." This only masks my neediness without addressing it. It is quite different from "I trust that I can find what I'm looking for within, so I release you." This is the true emancipation from neediness.

I may resent my partner for wanting me to treat them like a child. Of course, put in such a way, this sounds unreasonable. However, I can reframe the way I think of it: the little child in my partner wants to be acknowledged and responded to with unconditional love. Is this appeal unreasonable? The confusion may lie in assuming that if my partner is asking for love, I have to give it to them in the form their ego is requesting. Naturally, I respond to that with distaste, and pull back. What I'm overlooking is the possibility that I can offer love on my own terms without giving in to the neediness of their demands. This keeps my own boundaries intact and feels a lot better than not loving at all. Love always finds a suitable channel; its endeavors are invariably appropriate and helpful.

. . .

Is a peaceful relationship my goal? It's tempting to think so. But when I value surface harmony above all else, I relinquish the possibility of greater depth. I look at the great artists: they are always taking risks, with occasional failures inevitable. Beethoven's magnificent flops are the price of his lofty achievements. A pole-vaulter who always clears the bar is setting it too low.

The same is true in intimacy: if I never experience a major upheaval, I am probably paying a considerable price for this questionable and shallow peace. The outcome is likely to be dullness. Flatness or stagnation in my relationship indicates a lack of passion for exploring difficulties. It is a signal to me to have more courage, to be willing to rock the boat.

Do I have room in my heart for my partner to be identified with fear as part of their journey? The answer is often theoretically Yes and practically No. I am interested in the gap between the two.

All too often, I employ an unloving style in telling my partner to stop being negative. The response is predictably unfavorable. It's tempting to tell myself that they just can't handle honest feedback, they are in denial, and so on. Of course, they are simply a mirror for my own lack of love in the telling.

One of my ego's favorite myths is that I'm going to get you to love me more by blaming you for not loving me enough. If I want to increase the amount of love I receive, the only way that makes any sense is to offer more love. Without this essential step, I will spend a lifetime blaming others, wondering why I get so little in return.

Most of us desire a partner who shows us more or less continually that they want our happiness, while we reserve the right to blame them regularly for their many imperfections. In displaying a highly conditional love, we get upset with our partner for failing to love us unconditionally. Seeing this eliminates a lot of righteous judgment.

Hard experience shows me that offering spiritual or psychological insights when my heart is closed is never a good idea. If I am feeling resentment toward my partner, I may not want to ask them for any change until they trust that I wish them well. Even the slightest judgment conveys the message that they don't deserve love, which is all they would likely hear. If my goal is to be heard, then I am better off waiting until I can convey the message in a loving way. Love always knows what is appropriate. In the meantime, I allow others to inform my partner of their imperfections, and tend to my own instead.

Focusing on my partner's issues is a futile exercise. When I experience problems in my intimacy, it is always a dynamic for two rather than an issue for one. When I fail to acknowledge my own role in the dance, I give my partner the impression that I perceive them as the culprit. Admitting that I do many of the same things they do softens this impression. Even when they do something that I believe I wouldn't, I may still have a role in the dance. It may be the unloving quality of my response. Or I may simply have expressed unconscious negativity in a different fashion, or have done things unconsciously to trigger my partner's reaction. Perhaps my role is a general withholding of love, or feeling righteously superior to my partner. I may safely assume that I am always complicit in our negative interactions.

⟡

I expect my partner to trust me; I feel hurt when they don't. My taking offense is a sure sign of my own doubts about myself. Whenever I am clear about my own integrity, I feel no defensiveness when accused of its lack. Similarly, I may not trust my partner because I don't trust myself to wish them well. If I had unreserved goodwill toward them, it would be easy to imagine them feeling the same toward me. I tend to see others' feelings toward me as a projection of the way I regard them.

I may wish that my partner were more forthright about their feelings. It is natural to desire a loving environment wherein both partners feel comfortable sharing all their feelings with one another. Yet once again, Ego perverts this natural desire. I come to frown upon "withholding," as if it was a sin to avoid revealing all of one's truth in relationship. Of course I, myself, refrain from revealing my own truth whenever I don't feel safe in doing so. If I want my partner to be open to me, I need to take responsibility for creating a safe environment so they feel free to speak their truth without feeling my blame. I avoid conveying the double message that I want them to be impeccably honest with me, but that when they are, I reserve the right to blame. My partner will be more willing to speak their full truth if they know they won't be judged harshly for their human failings.

·   ·   ·

In my anger at my partner for withholding their truth, I perceive my own self-righteousness. I act as though I never keep things back. I forget all the times that I have withheld out of fear. I also harbor the false belief that my safety lies in having my partner's expressions of fear conform to what I approve.

⌐⌐⌐

Living intimately with my partner, I become acutely aware of their areas of guilt. Knowing this, I am tempted to use this knowledge as a way of influencing them to change. This is a poor strategy. While in the short run I may succeed in manipulating them, the resentment that inevitably follows will show that the price is not worth it.

Caught in my ego, I hear myself complain to my partner "Whatever I do, it's never enough." I would do well to examine honestly whether I am claiming that my partner is never loving and kind. Clearly they are sometimes loving. At such times, are they not saying that what I do is enough? Moreover, I am now doing the same thing I was complaining about by implying that their loving behavior isn't enough because it's not offered continuously.

Loving my partner unconditionally will do more to help them change than any amount of unloving attempts will.

I have a belief that I "need" my partner to be more loving, more sensitive, or more accepting. Is this really true? And do I serve the relationship by holding this belief? When I convey this message to my partner, I am suggesting that there is something wrong with them for not sufficiently being the way I wish them to be. This is scarcely a demonstration of my own loving acceptance. In truth, I don't need anybody to be different; that is merely the perception of my ego. But that does not mean that I cannot ask for anything. Although it is not reasonable to expect my partner to be anyone other than who they are, in a conscious relationship it is in our mutual interest to encourage each other to be a more conscious version of ourselves. This is best fostered in an atmosphere of mutual loving acceptance.

Is it reasonable to ask my partner to change? It is not only natural, but entirely appropriate for me to want to influence my partner's behavior. Clearly, I want them to know what works and what doesn't work for me. Of course I wish to do this in a way that is palatable to them. Whether or not I can do so depends on my state when asking. When I ask for change with an open heart, respecting my own needs but also loving my partner and wishing them happiness, it is rarely a problem. But my attempts to influence have quite a different effect when they do not proceed from love. To come to my partner with blame, resentment, or fear while attempting to change their behavior tends to elicit a stubbornness on their part, a lack of desire to please, a resistance to change. Only when they feel my respectful understanding will they be open to letting my feedback in. Even here, there are no guarantees. If I am unattached to results, if it is okay with me that they don't change, then my chance of influencing them successfully is maximized.

Before asking my partner to change, perhaps I might want to find out in what ways they would like me to behave more consciously. Then I will experience firsthand the inner obstacles to change, and perhaps understand more fully how difficult it is to alter deeply rooted behavior. I might be inclined to

cut my partner more slack when they don't change as fast or
as obligingly as I'd like.

How about when my partner tries to get *me* to change?
Instead of referring to their behavior with blame-laden words
such as "controlling" or "manipulating," I can view their
behavior as stemming from a legitimate, if perhaps unconscious, attempt to influence me. After all, isn't my wanting
them to stop doing it an attempt to control them? We all want
to have an impact on the behavior of others. It is simply more
honest and effective to do it as consciously as possible.

When my partner complains about my behavior and I
respond, with a shrug, "That's just the way I am," I display a
lack of discontent with my own imperfections. It is guaranteed
to arrest the lifetime process of maturing. Why do I allow this?
Because apparently my ego believes it would be a sacrifice. It
does not want to say "Yes, I do that. I can see how difficult I
can sometimes be for you. I would like to change." Though in
the abstract I wish to make a change in my relationship, my
ego resists. I postpone changing, usually with the fiction that
circumstances are too stressful right now. In truth, it never feels
like a good time. Yet any change I wish for has to happen Now.

⌒

Does it matter how conflict begins? I seem to believe so, justifying my negativity when it comes in retaliation. To say "You
started it" is so egregiously childish that I don't like to admit I
do it. Yet how often do I unlovingly accuse my partner of
speaking to me unlovingly. I feel I have such a right because
they did it first. But is there any real difference? Is my unloving behavior justifiable as long as I don't go first?

In relating, I continuously send forth signals arising either from my essential core or from an idea of how I think I should be or would like to be. What keeps me from expressing my core is a false belief that being who I am is unacceptable. This belief requires me to present a shell of personality. When the signals I send forth come from this shell, another set of signals—one I can't hide—arises from my unconscious core and clashes with my little act. Others are likely to experience this discord and feel uncomfortable being intimate with me. When I am at ease with myself, I am free of this contradiction; I send a single set of signals from my essence. This conveys more of the kind of presence and ease that encourages others to engage.

I feel comfortable with people who relate more from their essence. These are often young children, or people from more traditional cultures. But they also include people who seem to have less emotional baggage, either by temperament or because they have done a lot of work on themselves. When an interaction is inhibited and superficial, as when I meet some-one at a party and we reveal only the shells of our personali-ties, I often come away empty. When my essence meets that of another, I feel nourished.

Is it all right with me for the one I love to make a mistake or behave unconsciously? Or is it my job, in the interest of their well-being, to prevent them from doing so? One side of me convincingly asserts that their path is their own business. Of course they will make mistakes, and I can accept that. I know they will learn from them, as I have from mine, and I wish them well. On the other hand, I have a natural human desire to see those I care for be happy and healthy. If a skillful intervention can save them unnecessary pain, why not make it? Although both perspectives have truth, I usually go wrong in the direction of unskillful interference. My ego enjoys representing its need to control as a desire to help. The ultimate decision is best left to my Deeper Wisdom.

I see my partner doing something self-destructive. To what extent is this a concern of mine, and how do I handle it? The one approach to which nobody responds well is nagging. In an attempt to avoid that, I go to the other extreme, bottling up my feelings. In neither case am I able to be of any support. How do I discern if, when, and how to speak? First of all, I need to decide honestly whether I am personally and directly affected by the consequences of my partner's actions. If so, I have some reason to express my concern.

In a period of excessive caffeine use, I am asked by my partner to cut down. I am annoyed, feeling that it is none of their affair how much coffee I drink. But in truth, excessive caffeine often leads to irritability, especially at night, and my partner is objecting to having to live with my testy moods. The communication is an honest request; it makes no pretense of being made "for my own good." Because of this, it is easy for me to accept; I realize that my partner has every right to ask me to look at a habit that affects them so directly.

When I am not so immediately affected by my partner's behavior, the best response may be less obvious. If someone I love is following a path that will likely lead to pain, I may out of compassion look for an opening to intervene lovingly. There is nothing wrong with this; certainly if I were behaving unconsciously or unskillfully, I would wish my partner to inform me of it with an open heart. But the open heart is, of course, the key. If I am feeling annoyance with my partner over what they are doing, it is probably a sign that my ego has a stake in this. In that case, I'd best not offer advice or insights, and attend rather to my own imperfections.

If I approach my partner out of my own fear while asserting that I want them to be healthy and happy, I am espousing the teaching that fear is the road to happiness. They will intuitively sense something wrong with that and will likely resist. My fear—expressed often as blame—is not their best incentive. With faith that my own well-being is independent of my partner's behavior, I convey an ultimate message of safety: whatever form their life takes, I wish them well. Because my message is both true and free from judgment, they are more likely to be open to what I offer.

My partner asks me, "If I died, would it be okay with you?" I ponder what this "okay" means. I sense it is not "Would you grieve?" which my partner takes for granted I would. Rather, they ask "Is it fundamentally all right for me to die and for you to go through the natural pain of losing me?" If I answer No, I imply that they had better stay alive indefinitely for my sake. This is not very loving.

⁓

Do I have the capacity to be intimate only when I am energized or in a good mood? Is intimacy impossible if I am stressed out, tired, or grouchy? If I believe so, an opportunity is lost. Of course there are times when I prefer to be alone. Yet there are many occasions when an intimate connection can be nourishing, even though I feel less than good. When my energy is low, I can acknowledge it to my partner and just be a loving blob. When I am in fear or pain, I can share it without slipping into melodrama or self-pity. It is not necessary to shut my partner out; our intimacy can soften the edge of my discomfort and bring perspective. Indeed, it is a gift to my partner to offer all the colors in my emotional palette.

The intensity of the fear in my core determines how much spiritual teaching can be assimilated. As darkness becomes greater, the mind is less able to take in spiritual wisdom, however noble and true. When I am in the depths of my bleakness, words have little meaning to me. Only another's loving touch, or pure loving energy, has a chance of getting through to me.

When a fight or mutual resentment leads to a sullen wall between my partner and me, I may unfortunately allow it to persist for long stretches. Unable to muster the consciousness or determination to break out of my prison, I resign myself to the leaden, closed-down atmosphere. If my partner feels similarly, we are locked in paralysis. Our mutual resentment inhibits us both from making the first move. My ego says that I'm not going to initiate love, because if I do and my partner responds non-lovingly, what a humiliation that would be! I may even see reaching out in love after a quarrel as an admission of guilt; I will not be the first to "back down." The result is Ego's classic stalemate: "Let's be more loving . . . you go first."

I learn a great deal about myself by observing how my relationship with my parents intrudes into my present life. If my antennae are sensitive, I may notice countless fear-based attempts to please, moments of losing my equanimity, bursts of resentment—all of it quite familiar. If my parents are still alive, I have the opportunity to observe all this in the moment. If I reflect on it a bit, useful patterns begin to emerge. If I feel anger, fear, or neediness in the presence of my parents (or those who "stand in" for them), it seems likely that I am seeking their love and approval. If I obsess about them or engage in inner arguments, I have probably given them the job of defining my worth. If so, I will resent them for having such power over me.

My desire to feel self-worth is legitimate, but as an adult I can never find it from my parents. I could spend a lifetime trying to get my parents to give me what I want, or feeling aggrieved that they once didn't. Taking back the power to define my own worth, I can release my parents (alive or not) from being responsible for my present condition. When I do, I am well on the way to emotional adulthood.

Neither a parent nor anyone else has the power to make me feel guilty. Others may judge me, and I have the option to agree or disagree with their judgment. If I disagree (not just out of defensiveness, but at the core of my being), their opinion of me loses all power to bring me guilt or pain. This allows me to retain healthy boundaries. Out of self-compassion, I can determine the kind of environment I wish to inhabit, including the quality of relationships in which I am willing to engage.

I seek commitment from my partner and am frustrated because it is not forthcoming. What I may not realize is that I am asking for trust before that quality has been truly established. The best way of bringing more trust into a relationship is to demonstrate it. Perhaps I need to do so by trusting the slower rhythm of my partner. Perhaps they need to feel that the relationship has the capacity to deal successfully with conflict, especially around difficult issues, before they can commit fully.

Learning to create an emotionally safe climate in the midst of disagreements is more likely to lead to commitment than pressuring my partner to become committed. For me to push for commitment as a way of solving a presently uncomfortable situation makes no sense. Only when the basic feeling is positive and loving will it be appropriate to discuss commitment. Like many worthy goals, it is best obtained organically.

To love another is to want to make them happy. On the other hand, I know well that my own happiness cannot come from outside myself. It follows, therefore, that my partner's happiness cannot come from me. My wish to make my partner totally happy is impossible to fulfill; yet it perfectly expresses my love. I must live with that paradox.

My partner has an emotional wound, a tender area easily hurt. Fear tells me that I have to walk on eggshells as I draw near, which often leads to resentment. Love proclaims that I needn't ever walk on eggshells, only to approach with sensitivity.

· · ·

I think of doing something kind for my partner but then hesitate, feeling that it would be a sacrifice. This indicates that I am probably harboring major resentment. I may offer myself all sorts of reasons not to bend in their direction: for example, that what they desire is "irrational." This hides a simple truth: when I resent someone, I am not enthusiastic about doing them any favors.

Whenever I feel resistance to my partner's wanting something from me, I become conscious of how much importance I place on not giving it. It's not the particular favor I begrudge, but the very giving of anything to someone I am resenting. Once my resentments are released, I am usually happy to give my partner what they are asking for. Occasionally I may have a good reason not to, but in truth this seldom happens. By giving without the need to have any special reason, I send my partner the strongest possible message that I wish them well, namely, my willingness to demonstrate it through my actions.

If, when my partner is unable to give, I complain that I'm giving but not getting anything back, how pure is the quality of my giving? Weighing whether my partner is giving something back, or being sufficiently grateful, is Fear's version of giving. It is an expression of conditional love.

I inform my partner what I want or don't want from them, something important to me. They behave as if they haven't heard me or taken me seriously. I repeat myself, eliciting a similar response. What often happens next is a dramatic shift in style: angry at not being taken seriously, I blow up. Because they now feel accused and threatened, they may still not hear me, and if they do, it is with resentment. Clearly, a third alternative is called for.

If my first communication presents boundaries insufficiently strong for the circumstance, my explosion into anger produces the opposite difficulty: I close my heart and either anger or frighten my partner, which certainly fails to inspire their concern for my wishes. What is missing is a commingling of firm boundaries and an open heart. I realize that role models are scarce for such a combination, and I have to feel my way into it.

What does this look like in practice? Loving parents, neither authoritarian nor permissive, setting a necessary boundary, may demonstrate the flavor of it. I get my partner's full attention, which means neither of us is doing the dishes, driving a car, listening to music, or being busy with distractions. I look them in the eye, concentrating my energy like a laser with the focused intention to be heard, while still keeping my heart open. Focusing on what I would like rather than on what bothers me, I speak with a combination of authority and gentleness, expecting to be taken seriously: "I really want you to do what you say you're going to do. It's really important to me." I have found that such communication is overwhelmingly more effective than an intense display of emotion.

It is difficult to convey my feelings to my partner when I am upset. It can feel like a choice between two unsatisfactory alternatives. One is to speak my truth bluntly and harshly. I justify my closed-hearted communication by invoking my hurt or angry feelings; I use the latter as an excuse, as if being "authentic" were in itself some sort of gift. Not only do I close my heart; I inform my partner, articulately and at length, how their behavior "forced" me to close it. My other alternative, equally unsatisfactory, is to avoid conflict by swallowing my feelings. I tell myself that I am being noble, or spiritual, that I am not the sort of person who dumps their anger on other people. Or I convince myself that I'm not really upset. This tends to increase my resentment to an even higher level. In the long run, it results in even greater disharmony.

Is there another alternative? Is it possible to speak my truth with enough love that I can minimize my partner's upset? Only when I feel good about myself do I find it possible. Then I learn to find the emotional balance to be honest and yet communicate my difficult feelings with grace.

When I am brimming over with negativity, I am sometimes tempted to bring it to my partner aggressively. Because I am in this state, I overlook some very basic, common-sense questions. Is this a good time? Is my partner in a proper state to receive what I am saying? How many critical communications have I given lately? Have I flooded the airwaves with an over-abundance of negativity? Have I balanced criticism with acknowledgment and appreciation? How would I like to have similar information presented to me? Most important of all, is my heart open? Once I have established suitable conditions, I am far more likely to be heard and understood.

I am often faced with a choice of whether to blurt out my negative feelings, or to try and temper them with caution or discretion. Both approaches have their virtues. The positive side of blurting is its spontaneity and the willingness to take risks. The positive side of caution is caring how my words will affect others. On the other hand, the negative side of blurting is its potential insensitivity to the feelings of others, while the negative side of caution is an absence of spontaneity, along with the avoidance of potentially healthy disturbance.

I make my partner uncomfortable with a hasty and ill-considered outburst. It is not well received. In retrospect, I could probably have predicted in advance, had I paused to think, that they would have a negative response. Learning from this, I develop the intention to choose my words and approach more deliberately, based on the response I con-sciously wish to evoke. As I am about to indulge my old habit, I sense a warning signal, reminding me that I have the option of pausing before blurting. I discover how very many things are better left unsaid.

⌐‿⌐

I wish, in my intimate relationship, to stop being a slave to my emotional states. Out in the world, even when I am in a bad mood, I can usually find a way of relating to others with decency and respect. Yet with my partner I am willing to indulge my negativity. Doesn't my partner deserve at least the same decency as a client or colleague? The usual answer—that when I'm at home I get to relax and be myself—is a poor and unworthy justification for being harsh, curt, or mean-spirited with the one I love. I intend to make every effort to let my partner feel my respect, no matter how I'm feeling.

I also ask myself how conscious I am in responding to my partner's bad mood. Do I give them the quality I would wish from them when I am feeling down? My dismissive or annoyed reaction to their negative tone of voice is habitual and runs deep. It arises from my ego's muddled belief that they should always treat me with a consistency of respect that I myself am unable to muster. I can learn to reinterpret their mood as an expression of unhappiness, fear, or confusion that is always deserving of love.

As I am falling asleep, my partner taps me and says that I am breathing too loudly. I react with anger, demanding to know how I can possibly not have the right to breathe in whatever way I'm breathing. How logical—yet this feels good to neither of us. The next morning we revisit it. First I validate my partner's feeling: sure, if I'm disturbed by someone's loud breathing while trying to sleep, I'd be annoyed too, especially if I try to tell them about it and they get huffy. My partner is then in a better state to hear my truth, which goes back to my childhood. I'm doing something innocently and I am reproached for it. I feel unfairly squelched; I get angry. The present situation reenacts this in the extreme: I'm just lying there breathing, and even *that* isn't all right! Both of our responses make sense, given the context. Once again I learn that there are no right or wrong positions in intimate relationship, only the different feelings of the partners, each perfectly valid.

How do I accomplish the difficult task of putting my defensive ego aside when listening to my partner's anger or hurt? Anyone who has tried knows that if the issue is loaded, it can be one of the most challenging tests of emotional strength. I do have one powerful incentive. I wish to be understood by my partner when I am upset, which means that I want them to put their own feelings and perspective temporarily aside so they can truly hear me. Unless I am willing to give the same validation, I can't ask it of them.

Can an intimacy in which partners lack the mutual capacity to understand each other's upset be capable of any real depth? Some of the greatest opportunities for understanding arise from the most difficult interactions. I wish with all my heart to make maximum use of these demanding occasions. My desire and intention afford me the energy and persistence to master what is admittedly an arduous task: to understand my partner's feelings without defense. My reward is the sacred moments that this, alone, makes possible.

When I have difficulty validating my partner's upset feelings, I often fail to see that they have an important desire that's not being fulfilled. It behooves me to find out what that desire is, and to understand why it's so important. Failure to do this leads to a major source of resentment: the perception of not being taken seriously. Once I grasp what my partner wants and why it is important, it is but a short step to empathy; I can grasp why its nonfulfillment is so painful or frustrating.

⌒

The momentum of history presents me with the unequal dominant-submissive relationship, in which real intimacy is scarcely possible. In the dominant role, I take more seriously my own self-interest and do what I want without worrying about my partner. In the subservient role (actually a disguised form of self-interest), I regard my partner's needs as paramount, swallow my feelings, and avoid standing up for what I want: I do what my partner wants and lack care for myself.

·   ·   ·

Although superiority and inferiority sound like polar opposites, they are simply reverse sides of a single coin: unworthiness. My need to be either dominant or subservient arises from my feeling bad about myself; I require something from my partner to allay my discomfort. Such a relationship arises from our mutual insecurity; both of us are willing to play our unhappy roles. It inevitably leads us to the limitation and resentment inherent in all hierarchical relationship.

If I am the subservient member and I get angry with my dominant partner for being controlling or assertive, I have missed the point: I have chosen to be in an unequal relationship. The instant someone chooses not to be in that kind of relationship, they are free and can't be controlled. If I am comfortable in myself, I will relate from a stance of equality with everyone, free from issues of power. Whenever someone tries to relate hierarchically with me (from either end), it will neither bother me nor take effect.

I may naturally experience fear when I contemplate a relationship based on equality. Our culture has taught us little about balanced intimacy, so for most of us it requires learning and practice. If my partner and I wish to establish equality, then we will each agree to ask for what we want without demanding it. Each of us will take the other's preferences into account at the same level as our own. We will each develop comfort in saying "Here's what I want; how is that for you?" If I'm inclined toward the dominant role, I tend to omit the second half of this proposal. If I am submissive, I neglect the first half. It helps to know on which side I tend to err.

My partner and I inevitably face the normal dilemma of contradictory desires around money, sex, living situation, children, and so forth. The way things ultimately turn out is greatly affected by the purpose we both bring to negotiation. We end up with far greater satisfaction when we apply the strong intention: we are here to create as loving an environment as we can. This requires us to put our heads and hearts together and come up with something with which we are both happy and satisfied. Purpose determines outcome.

I sometimes experience resistance toward adopting this stance, believing it will lead to being taken advantage of. I am unaware that by my resistance I am essentially saying "I am after my own good and don't care about yours—but I'm angry with you for not taking my needs more into account." When the absurdity of this is seen, I can no longer complain about my partner's lack of cooperation.

Focusing on a solution before finding alignment is starting from the wrong end. I experience frustration when trying to "work things out" before my partner and I establish an emotionally safe atmosphere. No matter how skilled we are at communicating, it is difficult to proceed effectively without a feeling of goodwill underlying the disturbance, a sense of wishing each other well. Without goodwill, the feeling of "I want it to work for you too" is missing.

Toward creating mutual kindness, I may do something that gladdens my partner's heart. Taking simple pleasure in their well-being improves the relationship at least as much as working on the difficulties. With harmony between allies who seek a mutually favorable solution, an acceptable resolution is not far away.

⌒⟋

I view my partner as having a less well-honed intellect than mine, and relish the feeling of superiority. Here I am embracing several questionable assumptions: first, that my supposedly "superior" intellect makes me a better person; second, that a superior intellect helps me to more effectively get what I truly want; and most important, that the quality of my partner's intelligence is actually inferior to mine, rather than just different.

In feeling superior to my partner, I am unaware that such an attitude will be transmitted subliminally. My partner will feel disrespected, have less access to their own special quality of intelligence, and something in them will close down. My own intelligence would scarcely blossom around someone who dismissed it.

A blessing awaits me when I allow that my partner has something important to teach me, a kind of intelligence that can enhance mine because it is different and complementary. If I cherish this precious gift, my partner will appreciate themselves more and blossom. When I bless and honor my partner with all my being, they are helped to become the kind of person they want to be and I will reap nothing but grace.

⌒⟋

While singing or playing music with others (one of the most intimate activities imaginable), I note the similarity to the nuances of relationship. I listen not only to the sound of my

own voice or instrument, but to the others as well. I am looking to participate in a unified sound where my contribution is
an equal among several, blending with just the right volume
and intensity. Subtle variations in tempo, dynamics, and phras-
ing make it imperative that I be tuned in to the whole. I cannot move in reaction a millisecond later, but must respond
with my co-musicians absolutely together in the moment.

In relationship, as in music, the meaning and beauty lies in
each moment, not in where it is leading. Although there is no
goal, there is interest. Interest is the source of energy for being
fully present. Although the nuances are fascinating, it's the state
of mind needed to discover them—a quiet alertness—that I
find most engaging. Attention to energetic subtleties, whether
musical or emotional, requires that I go beyond my limited self
in the interest of a greater whole.

If I consider my life with my partner as a musical composition
played over a lifetime, then every time I address them harshly,
I am playing the wrong note or am out of tune. I would like
to play this music—the music of our relationship—as beautifully as I can. I especially want to transcend unconscious negativity, the single greatest source of needless discord.

An essential step on the path toward unconditional love is to
become aware of how often I am unloving. Like a novice
musician, I may at first need a teacher to inform me when I
play the wrong note. My partner is in a unique position to
do this, if I allow them this function. Their feedback helps
me to realize all the ways I slip into unconscious negativity.
Whenever I lose my attention, shift to automatic, or become
identified with my fears, the music suffers. Later, as my

"musicianship" ripens, I become my own teacher. I learn to sense on my own when I am playing out of tune. In that more agreeable stage, I can begin to worry less about hitting the right notes and focus on playing those notes more beautifully.

As my intimacy progresses through time, I learn that dissonance is not always something to be avoided. When I incorporate it skillfully into the whole, it can give meaning and depth to the harmony. My love broadens and intensifies when brought to a place where it previously seemed not to be. The discord in my relationship, when learned from, resolves itself into a greater harmony.

I wish for my partner to feel better about themselves when they see themselves through my eyes. If I don't earnestly crave to live with a partner who feels respected and honored, I haven't understood the essence of intimacy.

My relationship may or may not be flourishing, but as long as I'm playing my edge with it, it is always interesting. The edge resides in a healthy discontent with my own non-loving. Playing the edge means locating and challenging the beliefs that lead me to that place. My wish to experience love in the presence of non-love brings meaning and depth to what is otherwise uncomfortable.

Is it important for partners to share major interests? We tend to assume so. When intimacy becomes uncomfortable, the notion that "we don't have anything in common" is often cited as proof that the relationship cannot work. Yet if we understand what true intimacy means, we may find that it has little to do with sharing "interests" like music, sailing, or climbing the Rockies. Rather it happens at another, more basic level. To connect deeply, we need only enjoy being together. The simplest, most ordinary activities will do: lying in bed, sitting on the porch listening to the rain or watching it get dark, or strolling together on a quiet road.

Is it possible to find a common interest that does have a special importance? If so, it would surely be a shared sense of the relationship's purpose. If my partner's purpose is to use the relationship to wake up, but mine is merely to experience security and non-disturbance, the prognosis would seem rather poor. But when we come together with a spiritual goal, then whatever happens in our relationship can serve that goal—as long as we use it in that way. As we collide with each other, we learn swiftly and vividly about what gets in our way. Our relationship deepens and the Universe supports us in our struggles.

What does it mean to have a shared spiritual purpose? Does it mean we have to be in metaphysical alignment, read the same books, go to the same church or spiritual gathering? Or is it more like sharing a certain core sense of what is most important? Though words cannot adequately express it, an approximation of such a shared perspective might be: that there is a reality beyond the one we experience. It is possible and desirable to connect with that reality. An inner task exists which, if we can perform it regularly, will help us toward that end. We can be allies in helping each other to find the highest we are capable of. The events of daily life will bring us material to shine a light on the obstacles, in order to dissolve them. Learning to love more purely and unconditionally will bring us what we most seek in our lives.

⁓

If my relationship is honest, it will inevitably display the whole parade of normal human feelings. Yet it isn't necessary for me to retain the resentment that lurks underneath the surface fluctuations. If I investigate my periods of unlovingness with a healthy discontent, they become fewer, shorter-lasting, less solid and heavy. My glimpses of a loving state become more frequent and inspire me to keep at it. It may help to have the earnest persistence of Newton, who, when asked how he discovered the Law of Gravity, replied, "By thinking about it all the time."

My ego believes that having a partner who loves me is a crucial mark of my worth. If my unconscious purpose in pursuing intimacy is to get my partner to relieve my burden of uneasiness, then I look to them to establish that worth by loving me unceasingly. But, of course, they can't possibly fulfill this assignment; so whenever their love is hidden temporarily, I take this as evidence of my absolute unworthiness, and resent them.

Do I believe that my partner is here to remove my emptiness or pain? Who would want to acknowledge such a blatantly self-centered attitude? Yet I see how often I get upset with my partner when they are unloving. Does that not indicate that I do have such an attitude? If I believe that my partner can and should make me happy, then whenever they fail to fulfill their assigned function, they become the enemy and I resent them.

.   .   .

My partner's very unhappiness, which is not much different from my own, gives me still more reason to think worse of myself—if I were a better partner, they would be happy all the time. This is perhaps why I often resent the one I love simply for being unhappy. I wouldn't normally place these kinds of demand on a friend, so I have less need to resent them. Perhaps my easiest relationship of all is with my cat: I have all the room in the world for her to be a cat, which very much includes her aloofness. Imagine resenting her for that!

As long as I expect my partner to assuage my own feelings of unworthiness by providing me the love I cannot find within myself, what they give me will never be enough. I contemplate saying to my partner "I hereby absolve you from the task of making me happy, fulfilled, or secure; that's *my* job." I feel a certain resistance to doing that. If I follow this resistance, listening to what it is saying, I may uncover hidden expectations that are fueling my resentment.

When my ego is engaged, I assign others the duty to love me, entertain me, like me, interest me, comfort me, agree with me, be impressed by me, fear me, or perhaps not notice me. I can measure the importance of their role by how uncomfortable I feel in their presence.

If I released my expectations of others, I would have no reason to be ill at ease around them. Complete freedom from expectations is a vision, one perhaps not perfectly attainable. But being aware of my expectations, I can at least choose, in the moment, whether to continue carrying them or to let them go.

.   .   .

I tend to think of my relationship with my partner in terms of what I can get out of it. But is there a more productive way to view it? What if its purpose is not my own self-gratification, but rather to learn more about who I really am, to remain present while seeing what develops, to serve our common good, and to love as much as I can, given the reality of my fears? With such purposes I need harbor no hidden demands of my partner. They no longer exist simply to please me. As soon as I recognize this, the central source of my discomfort evaporates.

Good communication between partners surely goes beyond expressing what is being felt with accuracy and eloquence. If I resent my partner, then no matter how efficiently or articulately I convey my condemnation of them, I am still supporting the feeling that my partner doesn't deserve love. Such communication is ultimately ineffective.

Can I find a way to be honest about my negative feelings and, at the same time, more forgiving? It is quite a razor's edge. Of course I wish to feel comfortable being myself, with all my unpleasant reactions. Suppression or denial of my negativity destroys the integrity and depth of our intimacy. Yet emotional safety is absolutely essential to the health of our connection, and I wish to provide an atmosphere for my partner that is conducive to mutual trust, especially around sensitive issues. This safety is hard to come by in the presence of blame, or judgment.

.   .   .

Can I isolate judgment from the rest of my feelings? When I examine the workings of my mind, I see that judgment, or blame, is not a true feeling, but an aberration superimposed by thought. I support my anger by finding someone or something to blame. The blame is the smoke; the feelings are the flame that I wish to purify. Through awareness, I can create a smoke detector. Although I give myself permission to experience judgment and work with it, I don't communicate *from* my judgment. If I am too identified with judgment to do this, I postpone communicating until I can put some space around it. Relationship cannot flourish in the presence of judgment; no work on a relationship can be done without first contacting a place of love in the Now.

In any relationship, there is a healthy balance between introspection and engagement, as well as a natural movement between the two. After exploring my inner landscape in quiet solitude, I come together with my partner, allowing what I have learned to enrich our intimacy. By the same token, I bring what occurs in our interactions back to my solitude to be digested, deepening my self-knowledge. As the tide goes in and out, the two aspects balance and enrich each other. So the dance of relationship unfolds.

VI

OPENING

THE

HEART

Learning to open the closed heart is the most difficult task I face. Indeed, it is perhaps the most challenging mission for the human consciousness. All spiritual teachings agree that the goal is desirable; yet I see precious little to help me actually do it. Merely hearing the command "Thou shalt be loving" accomplishes little, and I see few models of open-heartedness in the world around me. So how do I go from having a closed heart to an open one? It seems to be a black-belt task of the first order.

Can I possibly be of benefit to the world when my heart is closed? Whatever is motivated by love feels good and helps the world; whatever isn't feels bad and creates strife. Does the world need my closed heart? Is my judgment making the world a better place? My life assumes order and direction when I understand that to be unloving is to be confused. I then let go of the notion that I have a rational justification for closing my heart to another.

Anything said without love is, in the deepest sense, giving the wrong message.

. . .

Either I attempt to figure out whom I can blame for this lack of love, or I can bring love to this moment. I cannot do both at the same time.

Since love always feels good, all uncomfortable feelings arise from a single source: the closing of my heart. The simple, eternally relevant answer to my feeling bad is to open the heart— to my bad feeling, and to everything else as well.

Most spiritual doctrines teach me not to pass judgment on others. Do I really accept this? I observe how frequently I continue to judge others: X is so unaware, Y has the wrong political opinions, Z is too self-centered. Justifying my judgments, believing I ought to judge, guarantees the persistence of judgment. The belief in the value of my judgment develops its first crack when I begin to suspect how unhappy the judge actually is. When I am passing judgment, I may enjoy feeling superior at one level, but beneath my superficial comfort I'm usually unaware of how deeply bad it feels to close my heart, how much energy it takes. This is perhaps easier to observe in someone else.

Judgment is toxic. It's not good for my health, it depletes my energy, it makes me less attractive, it perpetuates what I find distasteful in the world. How bothered am I by the fact that I do this to myself? If I am at all sensitive, I will find any manifestation of non-love in myself distressing. This pain can bring forth the gift of Divine Discontent, which motivates me to move toward Love. Sooner or later I understand that if I want to know peace and to have a positive effect on those around

me, my judgments must go. The first and perhaps most important step is to see clearly that eliminating judgment would be
an improvement.

I judge others for their "ridiculous" beliefs. I fail to realize that
whenever I adopt Fear's premise that safety lies in non-love, I
am embracing an equally "ridiculous" belief.

Fear knows how to distort Loving Truth on behalf of itself. A
voice within says "If you really understood this spiritual stuff,
you'd be a lot more loving and peaceful. The fact that you're
not proves that you're a phony." The grain of truth here is that
the test of my spiritual understanding will indeed be reflected
in my inner and outer behavior. But if I use that fact in any
way to make myself feel bad, then that simply means I have
misunderstood. Offering a spiritual perception with an unloving heart is tantamount to announcing "Here is a truth I don't
really understand." Any spiritual truth, if fully grasped, would
make me feel good. If, when I express it, I feel judgment or
negativity, that automatically means I haven't fully absorbed it.

I contemplate ending all judgment of others. Feeling my
resistance to doing this, I listen to what the resistance is saying.
The source of my suffering is now in full view. Holding on to
my justifications for withholding love is the great bottleneck
that constricts the heart from opening.

If I judge one person for one thing, then I am basically asserting the general validity of withholding love. I enjoy playing
God, deciding who deserves love and who doesn't. I decree
that the sun shine on this person but not on that one. I, who

am so often unloving, self-centered, insensitive, and petty, get
to decide that you are unworthy.

When I look beneath my judgments, certain unconscious
beliefs are regularly revealed as their source: You must earn
love by good behavior, always being emotionally mature and
loving. You have the power to hurt me by failing in your
appointed task. I never do what I'm accusing you of, and
therefore feel superior to you, which disproves my inadequacy.
And finally, the most universal belief: Closing my heart will
keep me safe.

Do I believe that judgment is "bad"? That sounds like a judgment.

I blame others for their unloving behavior, which I can usually
trace to their not feeling good about themselves. So I am actually blaming them for not feeling good about themselves. If
I believe that they are wrong in not feeling good about themselves, then I should logically be demonstrating that truth by
loving them. If I (falsely) think they are right in not loving
themselves, then I have no grounds to blame them for it. Either
way, I'm off base.

⁓

The intellectual person judges people based on their bril-
liance, their knowledge, or whether they are "right." The ma-
terialist judges them for their success in the world. The
"spiritual" person judges them for their perceived virtue, spiritual "advancement," or awareness. It helps to know where I
tend to judge others, as a first step toward stopping.

·   ·   ·

How do I justify my judgments to myself? What words do I say to give myself permission to judge myself or others? Certain words like "hypocrite" fairly drip with pejorative overtones. The word implies that we should all be consistent, and that anyone who isn't is bad.

I might be wise to embrace an attitude that accepts human imperfection, including my own. Everybody would get an A in such a class. My vision isn't to be perfectly free of Ego; I am not personally aware of anyone who is. It's easy to imagine even a fully awakened being who slips occasionally into Ego because of the thousands of years' worth of conditioning that lurks within our consciousness. Because they have trained themselves to look honestly within, they catch it quickly, see it for what it is, and don't judge it or make it bad; but neither do they allow themselves to be caught up in it. To the extent that they recognize quickly that they have gotten into Ego, it won't run them. That eliminates any problem that Ego might create.

I can learn to recognize Ego more quickly, smile at it, and take it less seriously. Whether I see Ego in myself or in others, I can refrain from seeing it as something to be gotten rid of. I feel more at peace with that as a vision than the ideal of being someone who never gets into Ego. Not only will I feel more comfortable with myself, but others will feel safer when they sense that all their expressions of ego are okay with me.

⌒

I find myself disapproving of someone else's behavior and I am convinced that I see their mistakes clearly. What am I telling myself: that I know exactly how others should live their lives, because I have lived mine so impeccably? Yet I can transform this absurdity into a truth. I have indeed led my life impeccably, doing everything I should, including my frequent bumbling and many egregious mistakes. Seen in the light of greater truth, my path does have a kind of perfection to it. Therefore, I do know how others should lead their lives: just exactly as they are doing.

A common spiritual lament is the wish that I could get rid of my judgments. When would that be? The notion that I'll indulge my unkindness now, but will somehow become kind in the future, is just another of Ego's strategies for its self-perpetuation. By postponing change to an imaginary time called "later," I get to keep living in the grip of uncounscious habit. Concerning myself with past or future judgments has no relevance. Am I willing to release judgment now?

I see that I can no longer legitimately pass judgment on anybody for anything, yet my old habit of judging plays itself out. The difference is that I am no longer able to support this habit. Although my judgments still arise, in ceasing to support the mind's endorsement of them I withdraw the food that sustains them. Over time, they begin to wither. My interest is not to be free of judgment arising; it is to cease justifying judgment once I am aware of its presence.

The actions that my ego blames arise not from loving behavior, but from fear. I judge others for their self-centeredness, insensitivity, failure to be tuned in to my needs, or not being blessed with my superior understanding. I even judge them—perhaps most of all—for being judgmental! At bottom, all of these judgments are fear-based.

• • •

The more fear-based expression I see in someone, the harder it is to love them. Does the fact that a person carries and expresses a lot of fear put them in the category of one who doesn't deserve love? You don't get love if you're too afraid?

Ego insists that some forms of fear-based behavior are worse than others. It may be useful to be clear about exactly which forms of fear-based behavior I believe don't deserve love. How do I decide who does and doesn't deserve love, and under what circumstances? One person withdraws, another acts greedily, another gets angry or violent, another goes into denial, another becomes arrogant, another behaves like a victim, another puts on a sugar-coated mask, another avoids pain through the use of chemicals. Chances are that I am more upset by certain of these than by others. Do young children all deserve love? If so, is there some point in their life where this no longer holds? Could it be that my ranking system is somewhat arbitrary and subjective?

I seem to believe that my particular way of manifesting fear is superior to another's. The only reason such an absurd assumption persists is that I haven't sufficiently challenged it. Upon investigation, I understand that all fear-based behavior, no matter how unsavory or wide-ranging, arises from one source. It either all deserves blame or all deserves compassion. In assigning blame, I fail to see that my assumption of superiority is fear-based behavior. The ego is a kitten that loves to chase its tail.

⌒

Since judgment comes from a place of moral superiority, it would seem worthwhile for me to establish whether or not I am, in fact, morally superior. If I myself were free of all fear-based behavior, I wouldn't feel morally superior to anybody. What, then, would happen to my judgments? Perhaps I would be forced to take my stand that everyone deserves love always. Perhaps I can take that stand anyway.

I see others playing the role of spiritual teacher, unaware of their ego, and judge them harshly. I admonish myself that if ever I dare play the role of teacher, I'd better have my act together. But then, in my own teaching, I display many holes in my own awareness. Of course, I judge myself unmercifully for this. However, when I come to accept myself as a teacher who sometimes gets into ego, who makes mistakes, who is capable of acting foolishly or without awareness, I am no longer bothered by others manifesting those same imperfections.

It is valuable for me to see the traits in others that trigger my judgment, as this shows me where I haven't forgiven myself. Sometimes it takes a bit of digging, because the traits that bother me in others are sometimes ones I fail to recognize in myself. In such cases I may be dealing with a quality that I don't express directly but would unconsciously like to. For example, I judge someone for being overly dramatic, while noting that I myself am not given to that particular excess. Nevertheless, if I am honest, I see there is a part of me that would like to express itself dramatically, though I am too shy to do so. I am judging part of myself I don't normally allow into my awareness. My need to feel superior may represent an area of conflict within.

· · ·

There is an art in finding my own particular version of the traits for which I judge others. For example, I look with disdain on those who go jogging with iPods. I take pleasure in the thought that I do not do so. But I can no longer maintain this stance once I realize I have my own private, earphone-free iPod—my ceaseless inner monologue.

It is tempting to believe that I don't judge others, simply because my mind doesn't run to obviously judgmental thoughts like "What an idiot." But judgment need not be expressed as a conscious thought; it can be recognized by other signs, such as a diminishment of affection or kindness, a desire to avoid, or a greater tendency to find flaws.

I may believe that my not wishing another well is based on their unloving behavior or "wrong" beliefs. But upon investigation, it becomes plain that it's based entirely on my ego's interpretation that the other is my enemy. Ego sees everyone as part of either the self or the not-self. Once it determines the other to be the not-self, it decides to see the worst in them. Their words and actions are now used as an excuse to justify my preexisting judgment. Were I to see them as my ally, I would have no urge to close my heart, even when they do something I don't like. This explains my double standard for the same behavior with different people.

When I follow my belief that others don't deserve love to its source, I see that I am actually asserting "You don't deserve to live," which is, underneath it all, a gesture of violence.

Murder is simply the physical expression of this impulse, intensely amplified, but no different in kind from denying the other love. I may have trained myself not to kill my enemy, but withholding love is a gesture arising from the same violent source.

⁓

A young child is swinging a large branch about him. Unaware of my proximity, he hits me in the stomach with it. I feel an immediate, visceral burst of anger from having the wind knocked out of me. However, as soon as I look at the child, my first thought is that he didn't mean to hurt me. The animal anger lingers briefly but is not directed at the boy. Then that, too, fades and all is well. Never have I had clearer proof that I first decide what I want to see in another, and then see it. The decisions are made unconsciously. If I can make them conscious, then perhaps I can decide to see only beauty and goodness.

⁓

My ego loves to complain to others, "Look at you: you're more concerned about how you feel than about how I feel!" What am I doing in that moment? Plainly, being more concerned about how I'm feeling than about how you are feeling. In the process of blaming you, I commit the very act I find distasteful. That's what egos do.

I see myself judging my partner on a long trip for not being able to go with the flow when we have an unexpected delay. I laugh when I realize that blaming them for that is not going with the flow.

• • •

Righteousness is Ego's twisted version of the wish for peace. It mistakenly employs the violence of judgment as a means to a peaceful end.

My ego, in looking to justify my judgment of others, believes they are their ego. I assume that while I may also have an ego, mine is somehow better. Such self-righteousness requires that I be blind to myself. It is embarrassing to see how superior I feel whenever I pass judgment.

I am probably not wise to employ thou-shalt's and thou-shalt-not's as a way of escaping the trap of righteousness. These have been historically most ineffective. What is effective is to regard my own inner landscape with unwavering honesty, yet without guilt. When I observe my words, my actions, and (especially) my thoughts, I see how often I am self-centered and insensitive to others. How judgmental I am, how petty, how swift to blame and slow to forgive. If I have any doubt, I ask myself whether I would mind having all my thoughts broadcast uncensored on nationwide radio, for even an hour. If, despite my distaste, I persist in observing my innermost thoughts, the fruit of my awareness is to see my ego in its undisguised glory. The result is a kind of organic humility, the antidote to self-righteousness.

All egos are fundamentally the same. Those who believe otherwise display an inadequate knowledge of themselves. As Gurdjieff once put it, those who aspire to self-knowledge, look within, and aren't horrified by what they see, haven't really looked.

•   •   •

Gurdjieff also reminds us that if one is in prison, the single most important step in getting out is to realize that one is in prison. The most essential movement toward opening my heart is to realize how much it is closed. I need to be un-flinching in seeing the fact of it without self-judgment, denial, or justification. It comes to this: either I see my ego as the same as everyone else's, or I remain blind to the obvious.

⌒

Do I believe that others should always be respectful to me? If I do, and they are not, I close my heart to them. My message is that they deserve love only when they behave as I wish. Is that respectful?

When I judge someone for their actions, I rarely consider that I may do the equivalent. I'm not likely to say "I do it too; we're both bad." Maintaining judgment depends on my feeling of superiority. The implication is: "You do that, but I don't. That makes me better than you." My conviction that "I don't do that" arises from having too narrow a definition of "that." When I see someone else behaving unconsciously, I can feel superior to them as long as I don't behave unconsciously in that particular fashion. I may do it in my own way (such as in judging others). But I can't acknowledge that feeling of supe-riority directly to myself, because I would be appalled. In fact, that would be a downright "inferior" thing to do. In the very act of closing my heart, I would be demonstrating that I'm not morally superior to anyone. My ego prefers not to notice this.

It is useful to train myself, whenever I judge someone, to ask whether I do the same thing, perhaps in a different form. Or have I ever done it? An answer of "No" suggests that I haven't looked deeply. For example, I judge my partner for leaving a mess. In the meantime, I have all kinds of unfinished business in my own life—unforgiven people, loose threads of negativity, projects delayed, and so on—which is my own "mess." Indeed, the more I look, the more I see that everything I object to in another's behavior can be found in my own outer and inner life, though perhaps in altered form. Once I realize that I am just like the one I judge, then either we both deserve righteous judgment or we both deserve understanding and forgiveness. A fundamentalist attitude might be close to the former, proclaiming us both sinners. I prefer to take my stand in the latter.

I hear someone professing more enlightenment than their life displays, and find myself judging them. My ego is too canny to deny that I do the same thing. It says, instead, "Yes, I do that, but not nearly as much or as badly." Righteousness proclaims that I may be a bit self-centered, judgmental, or unloving, but you are beyond redemption!

One sign of righteousness is the phrase "How could you . . . ," which, of course, isn't really a question at all; it really means "I would never . . ." My righteousness may exclaim "How could that politician be so dishonest?," assuming that were I in a position of power, I would be a paragon of rectitude. I haven't cared to acknowledge the subtle ways my own honesty is open to question.

The particular area where my righteousness blossoms is a useful indication of where I haven't forgiven myself. If I judge someone for being greedy about money, then I am probably uncomfortable about my own greed, either about money or something else. Or I see someone who claims to be a spiritual authority unawarely putting people down. Without realizing it, I feel spiritually superior to them—in an equally unaware way. In both cases I am looking at a disowned part of myself.

I catch myself judging a friend for watching afternoon soap operas. I feel morally superior because I, myself, don't watch junky TV shows in the middle of the day. This is hard to admit to myself. Why? Perhaps an unacknowledged part of myself would like to do something similarly "dissolute." Or perhaps I already do the equivalent in disguised form. At least one thing is clear: I'm certainly not one who invariably uses his time well. Once I admit this, it's hard to support my feeling of superiority.

Instead of being caught up in my judgment, I now have some space around it: "There goes Ego doing its judgment again, but that's not me. I want to wish everyone well, even those who escape from their fear through food, drink, sex, fantasy, and, yes, junky TV shows."

The feeling of moral superiority that lies behind judgment is dissolved with humility. This elusive quality can't be achieved by direct effort. It arises as a natural consequence of seeing my own ego behave just like everyone else's.

⌒

One of Ego's most pain-producing tenets is that I should be eternally victorious in the battle of Life. When I am not, the belief that I have failed brings me the disgrace of defeat: not being properly loved, not being taken sufficiently into account, being insulted, embarrassing myself through mistakes, being wrong, not succeeding in love, sex, business, or health. These are heavy burdens to bear.

A major source of defeat occurs when, through honest self-observation, my pretense of superiority clashes with the reality of my ego. The destruction of my pretense elicits a moment of humiliation, against which I have habitually struggled through denial, anger, justification, self-pity, and judgment of others.

Ego believes that the less of defeat I suffer in my life, the greater I am. But nothing could be further from the truth. True greatness arises to the degree that I acknowledge the humiliation of defeat honestly, with dignity and poise, without embellishment and coloring, without humbug. Humiliation, neither fought against nor indulged in but accepted and digested, transmutes into humility.

Ego, founded on the false belief that it is special, continually seeks to maintain itself through feeling superior. When that's not possible, inferior will do. Its subtly disguised version of humility is to find satisfaction in accepting one's low place ("I'm just a poor slob," or "a poor sinner"). Taking pride in being less merely inverts the traditional vertical scale while retaining its essence. This is why humility can never be attained through an effort to be humble. It arises only as a byproduct of releasing verticality, the belief in "better" and "worse."

How often has my advice been unwelcome because of my lack of humility in giving it?

One of the fundamental questions of human relationship is whether it is okay to be non-loving. My understanding of psychology tells me Yes; my understanding of traditional spirituality tells me no. Both are right; both are wrong.

I wish to be a loving person, yet in fact I frequently close my heart. To open my closed heart requires balancing masculine and feminine spiritual energy. Healthy "feminine" spirituality surrenders to what is, lovingly embraces the entire content of consciousness, pleasant or otherwise, and releases fear in the process. Unless I accept all expressions of who I am, I close my heart to myself, tightening the knot even more and adding guilt to my list of difficulties. In order for any part of myself to change, I must first embrace it. Children's behavior isn't improved by yelling at them and making them bad; it's improved when they are first loved. Judging my ego as bad has the same effect; it is a pitfall that I risk when my spirituality lacks its feminine component.

I experience healthy "masculine" spirituality as my capacity to choose my attitude toward what is, concentrate my attention where I wish, and stay focused on my highest aspirations. The masculine aspect of my being holds a less accepting attitude toward my persistently closed heart. It is simply not okay with me that I spend the rest of my life unloving. I can do better than that. Divine Discontent is required to free myself from this petty ego state that brings me so much pain. This force is also necessary if I am to transcend the violence and suffering in this world. The absence of this "masculine" quality leads to complacency, a lack of motivation to ripen into the fullness of love. This is the typical pitfall of a purely psychological approach. All the psychological knowledge, tools, and techniques in the world are of no use to me unless I am aware of whether or not my heart is open and dissatisfied when it is not.

The answer to fear-based feminine energy—passivity, resignation, or victimhood—is healthy masculine energy expressed as strength, intention, or will. The answer to fear-based masculine energy—resistance, aggressiveness, or violence—is healthy feminine energy, whose essence is gentleness and acceptance.

I am tempted to take the feminine attitude of tolerance toward my own ego, and the masculine attitude of dissatisfaction toward the egos of others. It feels more productive to do the reverse. Or, even more so, to take the all-accepting feminine perspective toward others, and a healthy mixture of acceptance and Divine Discontent toward myself.

⌒

When feeling bad about myself, I am tempted to adopt the "spiritually correct" attitude that says everything is okay, including so-called negative emotions. At some level everything, indeed, is "okay." However if I really believed that, I wouldn't have created those negative feelings in the first place. My well-ensconced belief that things are not okay breeds resistance to what is, generating anger, hurt, and fear. On top of that, I intellectually impose the notion that "everything is okay." It is not very convincing.

I hear the spiritual exhortation to love what is, which sounds deeply true. Then a serious doubt arises, based on taking the dictum to mean that I look at what is and love its content, no matter how distasteful. I imagine living in the time of slavery and watching a master beat a slave unmercifully. Love that? Impossible!

Yet another meaning presents itself to me. I see loving what is as feeling a love in my heart that greets indiscriminately whatever lies before me. Should that turn out to be actions based in fear, my love is especially needed. Not only the slave, but even the violent master is in need of compassion. When I am in such a state, the particular content of the moment ceases to have importance; I can be present in the midst of the most disharmonious circumstances while centered in Loving Truth.

$\backsim$

I close my heart to my intimate partner. They remind me that I'm not being loving, with the result that I find my heart closing even more. Although it is true that we are mutually trying to create a more loving relationship, my ego distorts that into "It's wrong of me to close my heart," and their reminder becomes an accusation. The truth is, my heart *is* closed—fighting against that merely strengthens the contraction. Perhaps it would make things easier for my partner if I said "My heart is closed now, and I'd like to find a way to open it." It would be equally helpful to me if they could say "Of course I'd like your heart to be open to me, and it's okay that it isn't."

I fail to release past resentments for one reason only: I don't want to. My desire to hold on to them is at that moment greater than my desire to let go of them. It's that simple.

$\backsim$

Can one speak of oneself as a recovering intellectual? I look back on myself as a young man, worshipping at the altar of intellect, assigning worth to people on the basis of what they think. I distinguish between those whose opinions and tastes are "correct" (meaning: like mine) and those whose aren't, dismissing the latter as unworthy. But then I begin to notice that those who are facile thinkers seem no happier than anyone else, and are, in fact, often more troubled. It becomes plain that the thinking mind cannot create the level of change needed to be at peace. The pendulum swings to the other side, and for a time I dismiss the intellect as useless or worse. Finally this, too, comes to seem like an impasse, paralyzing rather than liberating.

Coming into maturity often reveals the pendulum's natural tendency to settle in the middle. Although intellect can play a role in fulfilling our deepest yearnings, its role may not be what we imagine when we operate from the thinking mind alone. A major value of our intellect lies in helping to open the heart. It can do this by locating and challenging the beliefs and assumptions that give rise to suffering. There is no need to feel conflicted; every part of my being has its function in the quest for a meaningful life.

Although it is tempting to regard mind as the problem, it is more helpful to see it as neutral. Fear can use it in a fearful way, and Love can use it lovingly; in itself it is neither good nor bad. It is not the mind, but Fear that is the problem.

Most of our daily thought stream is fear-based. To the extent that the mind's dominant vibration is fear, the movement toward love is impeded. But that same mind, inspired by Love, can be employed helpfully in the service of Truth.

My happiness is intimately connected to whether or not my heart is open. As long as the mind relentlessly closes the heart, suffering is guaranteed. If my wish is to feel good, this is not very intelligent. By observing how unintelligently I have lived my life until now, I make it hard for myself to feel intellectually superior.

In the midst of a strong negative feeling, I ask myself if I could push a button and suddenly feel love instead, would I easily and gladly choose that? The answer is no: I feel irrationally reluctant to let go of the feeling. What is that reluctance saying? "If I were to release this feeling, then . . ." What comes is that I wouldn't be safe. In its baldest terms, Fear starts with the premise that I am not safe and concludes that I can be made less unsafe by withholding love.

Ego has everything backward. Its insane premise of safety through non-love has been the guiding principle of warfare, of global economics and politics, of strife within cities, neighborhoods, and families, of conflict in intimate relationships, and of the turbulence in my own troubled mind. I am continually demonstrating to myself and to the world which belief system I choose to take my stand in: Ego, or Loving Truth. Do I do it consciously or unconsciously? Until now, I have been doing it mostly unconsciously.

If I am unconscious, then Ego's choice is made for me by default. Why would I want that? My belief that it's not safe to love is at the core of my suffering; it is why no amount of pleasure or experience can ever bring me the satisfaction I crave. Yet I am offered an opportunity to make another choice if I care to. It is not hard to see which choice makes sense. Once I begin to mistrust Ego's sanity, its power over my thoughts and behavior is limited. To recognize Ego's insanity is to set foot on the path to sanity.

If I hold resentment toward another, either I believe that I'm more loving than they are or I recognize that I'm not. If I resent them because I think I'm more loving, then I am unlovingly asserting "I'm more loving than you." If I acknowledge that I'm just as unloving, then I admit that I'm resenting them for being as unloving as I am. This is just one more reason to doubt Ego's sanity.

Someone sees a lost child crying by the side of the road and slaps them for being lost. What could be more insane? Yet is that not what I do whenever I close my heart to someone who is in a state of fear? And, most painfully, I do it to myself.

A major step toward love is to be both supremely aware of the suffering inherent in my closed heart, and sufficiently bothered by it.

If I pay attention, I can become conscious of the moment of choice just preceding the closing of my heart. Only when I am conscious do I have a true choice to stay open. As I practice making that choice it becomes increasingly effortless.

I say to myself "Unconsciousness is okay in a child, but I am an adult. I should be beyond that by now." I am forgetting to accept the natural rhythm of a ripening awareness, one that flowers earlier in some areas and later in others. Although my process may not be yet complete, I learn to trust in its pace. In so doing, I trust in the pace of others as well. I needn't impose my own tempo on another's ripening. I am willing to give others the right to learn what they need to at their own speed. I can relax and trust the timing of things. My impatience with others is merely my forgetting that everything happens according to its own rhythm.

⁓

Does my heart close the way the wind blows, something that just happens to me, over which I have no control? Or does it close because my mind makes a decision to close it? If the latter, the decision must be made beneath the level of conscious awareness. The mind must believe that a closed heart is its only option for safety.

Generally I don't get angry and blaming unless I believe that another has the power to hurt me. The notion that I must close my heart to protect myself against being hurt deserves my profoundest skepticism.

It becomes increasingly clear to me that the closing of my heart is not something done to me, but something I do. My deepest conditioning, beginning perhaps in infancy, has taught me that it's usually not safe to be loving. Unaware that there is another choice, I have heeded my unconscious mechanical training without a challenge, failing to perceive the painful consequences for myself and others.

·   ·   ·

When my heart is open, I feel good; I suffer only when my heart is closed. Does anyone else have the power to make me close my heart, and therefore to make me feel bad? I spend a lifetime blaming others for something that I, alone, have been doing to myself. Then I see that I no longer have to. What a relief!

How do I wish to behave toward others if I am conscious of feeling closed down? Clearly I wish to be neither indulgently negative nor artificially nice. Think of a musician or an actor having an off day, a bit out of-sorts, but facing the need to perform. Simply by making a clear decision to do so, he or she supplies a somewhat mechanical but passable version of an inspired performance. It's not quite the real thing, but it suffices.

Similarly, I possess a mechanical backup system that I can employ with others when my natural love or kindness is shut off. Activating it requires that I be aware enough of my closeddown state that it doesn't run me. And then I do the best I can. I don't pretend to feel better than I do, but I act with decency and respect—a mechanical version of love. In other words, I behave "as if." Sometimes it leads me toward genuine openheartedness.

I am more likely to employ mechanical civility in the world than at home, as if I believed "honest" negativity is more suitable to my family than courtesy. Perhaps I am confusing decency with the phoniness of an artificial "niceness," which I naturally wish to avoid. The conscious choice to be respectful when I am closed down is not as satisfying as true open-heartedness, but it feels preferable to indulging in mechanical disrespect.

~~~~~~

Is it a sacrifice to love others unconditionally? My first answer might be that of course it isn't. Yet I often behave as if I believe it is. Perhaps my hidden belief is what allows me to accept my own persistent holding back of love. If I have a strong unconscious pull to go south, I'd better deal with it if my true desire is to go north.

One of the biggest obstacles in learning to love unconditionally is the belief that it is possible for someone, at certain times, not to deserve love. Here is the perfect excuse for justifying the closing of my heart. Whenever I justify closing my heart to another, I am taking my stand that they deserve love only some of the time. Although I claim to love another person, I seem unaware that my conditional love is not really love, but rather an attempt to get something from them. This strengthens the false notion that another's behavior is a legitimate excuse for cutting myself off from my Source of life and joy. By continually affirming this untruth, I sink deeper into the illusion at the root of my suffering.

There is a vast difference between justifying the closing of the heart and accepting my closed heart but refusing to justify it. The first implies that another doesn't deserve my love because of the way they have behaved. The latter (they do deserve love, even though I'm not able to give it now) is a tentative but indispensable first step toward unconditional love.

.   .   .

Once I suspect that others deserve my love all the time, even when they act out of fear, I wish to determine honestly whether I have any reservations. Do I fear loving unconditionally? My reservations persist because of my unwillingness to hold deeply embedded beliefs up to the light of awareness, to apply focused skepticism. Exploring why I hold back from offering unconditional love is a major step toward achieving it.

The times when I am closed present the opportunity to get in touch with my belief that it's unsafe to love. While sitting peacefully, I may imagine a person with whom I'm having trouble. I can picture their tone of voice or a certain harsh look. I may recall some unfair criticism of me, or a failure to meet my desires. I experience my usual reaction. Then I contemplate wishing this person happiness and responding with unconditional love in spite of all. The prospect normally elicits a serious discomfort. In my resistance, I am now in direct touch with my feeling that it's not safe to love.

Going further, I ask myself what I am afraid of, what reason does Fear give for asserting that I can't love here? "Speak, Fear," I say. "I wish to hear your doubtless excellent reasons why I am better off keeping my heart closed." This brings me face to face with the core belief that says "It's not safe to love now because . . ." I listen openly to Fear's reasons.

For example, Fear may tell me that to love is to risk being engulfed, to lose myself. Having poor boundaries, I may believe that I can be either loving or strong, but never both. Or Fear may warn me that the other might reject my offering, and then I would feel hurt. This assumes the false premise that my hurt arises from another's rejection, rather than from my choosing to take offense. Often Fear, to justify my keeping a closed heart, assures me that the other doesn't deserve my love. Or Fear may assert that unconditional love will merely encourage unwanted behavior.

In all cases the "Love" that Fear has in mind is conditional. Love is seen as lacking boundaries, as weakness, as something undeserved, or as encouraging negative behavior. But real love—unconditional love—is none of these. It is fearless, feels neither rejection nor hurt, is given freely without being "deserved," and elicits more positive behavior. Perhaps Ego simply can't envision unconditional love or its profound rewards; it perceives the price as too high, the sacrifice too great. Yet from my deepest place of Truth, I know that Ego is wrong. No matter what it tells me, if I investigate my reasons for believing that it's not safe to love, they cannot withstand the light.